T0044552

Mental Health at Work

James Routledge is the Founder of Sanctus, a purpose-driven organization with a mission to put the world's first mental-health gyms on the high street. Sanctus partners with businesses to support employee mental health through proactive and preventative coaching. James founded Sanctus after his own experiences with poor mental health, which he began writing about, sharing his story on social media. Since then, he has built a strong following and Sanctus has grown to partner with hundreds of businesses, supporting tens of thousands of people with their mental health at work. His work has been featured in *The Times*, the *Guardian*, and on BBC TV and radio. James is a regular public speaker, writer and commentator on mental health, culture and entrepreneurship.

James Routledge

Mental Health at Work

BUSINESS

PENGUIN BUSINESS EXPERTS

UK | USA | Canada | Ireland | Australia
India | New Zealand | South Africa

Penguin Business Experts is part of the Penguin Random House group of companies whose addresses can be found at global.penguinrandomhouse.com.

Penguin
Random House
UK

First published 2021
002

Text design by Richard Marston
Set in 11.75/14.75 pt Minion Pro
Typeset by Jouve (UK), Milton Keynes
Printed and bound in Great Britain by Clays Ltd, Elcograf S.p.A.

The authorized representative in the EEA is Penguin Random House Ireland, Morrison Chambers, 32 Nassau Street, Dublin D02 YH68

A CIP catalogue record for this book is available from the British Library

ISBN: 978-0-241-48682-5

Follow us on LinkedIn: https://www.linkedin.com/company/penguin-connect/

www.greenpenguin.co.uk

MIX
Paper from responsible sources
FSC® C018179
FSC
www.fsc.org

Penguin Random House is committed to a sustainable future for our business, our readers and our planet. This book is made from Forest Stewardship Council® certified paper.

No book on mental health can be written without support. I dedicate this book to my fiancée, Sarah, who continues to grace me with love, light and support every day.

Contents

Introduction

I have no idea how to introduce myself. This page has created a lot of anxiety for me. I'm fearful of being judged. I'm imagining this book being left on a shelf to gather dust, or used as a coaster. That's my experience – and to not share it, in a book about mental health, feels false. To dive in, puffing my chest out and saying I feel 'fine', I'm 'all good' would be trite. Introducing myself here to you, I notice that as I give voice to my nervousness, I feel more settled, I can feel my feet on the floor, I feel more present and I feel my heart beating ever so slightly less quickly.

I know what it's like to be completely new to the subject of mental health, both within and outside work. I know what it's like to take this topic into the workplace and feel like it's just you, alone. I'm still here, doing it. At the time of writing this, I've been building a mental health business called Sanctus for the last five years. In that time we've partnered with hundreds of the world's biggest businesses, consulted with thousands of employees in workplaces of all shapes and sizes, and supported tens of thousands of individuals to improve their mental health. We've created unique spaces for people to work on their mental health in ways that are accessible, playful and creative. There are lots of stories to tell and lots of brilliant businesses, leaders and advocates to celebrate.

I'm still in the thick of building that business today, motivated by the desire to have an even greater impact and to bring about a transformation of mental health at work.

I'm trying to get other people to listen to me about mental health, while still understanding my own mental health too. I've faced many challenges when leading a business, not least battles with my own feelings of inadequacy. Working within the field of mental health, I have had plenty of experiences of not feeling credible, not feeling good enough, and succumbing to what many people describe as 'imposter syndrome'. I know what it's like to feel ill-equipped to deal with mental health, to be scared, lost and confused. To feel embarrassed for feeling how you're feeling; to feel like there is something wrong with you, but knowing that there's not. I know what it's like to suffer, and I know what it's like to have a curious excitement about mental health too.

Picking up this book is a step on your mental health journey, and you've chosen to do that in my company. I'm honoured and excited to do this together. It can be uncomfortable work – but rewarding too, and maybe even fun.

The fun is that neither you nor I know where this will lead.

So let's begin.

Part 1 My Story

1 Let's start at the beginning

When I reflect back on where mental health sat in my childhood, I see mental health everywhere: in my family, friends, all around me. With hindsight, I see how my life was shaped by the experiences and environment at the time, and I can see how pervasive mental health has always been. Yet as a child, teenager and young adult growing up, if you'd said the words 'mental health' to me, I wouldn't have had any idea what you were talking about. I don't recall the concept at all as a child. When I was growing up, if someone died, got married or there was some form of heartbreak, those were the few times I really remember emotions and feelings being allowed and, to an extent, encouraged. My experience is true for many of us still today.

Our emotional state and felt experiences are not always welcomed and are not woven into our daily lives. In fact, people who are more naturally in tune with their emotions are often labelled as 'emotional', 'crazy', 'erratic'. An emphasis on the felt experience is typically labelled as bad and 'counterproductive'.

Until my mid-twenties, my approach to life was to conform; I learned early on that expressing myself was a dangerous game to play (at school, in particular) and I wasn't brave enough to risk it. I concealed my interests in drama, music and art, hiding behind a fear of failure and judgement. Luckily for me, I excelled in school at the academic subjects and sports. For any young man, this acts as a free pass. Through this, I learned that certain parts of me were 'allowed' and other parts were not. On reflection now, the divide is quite clear: anything deemed 'masculine' was readily accepted with open arms, while anything even close to being described as 'feminine' was prone to judgement. So conformity won. Vulnerability, creativity, art, emotions, displaying love and affection openly: I put all of them off the table and repressed those parts of myself, until I could no longer function.

As a young, white man growing up, this approach to life presented absolutely no problems for me – indeed, it granted me incredible opportunities. If I had grown up as a woman or a member of the BAME community – essentially, anyone who isn't a white male – my experience would have been very different and I'd most likely have found it even more difficult to express myself. If I have found it hard to open up, share my feelings and talk about my mental health as a white man, then how hard must it be for those with fewer of those systemic and social privileges given to them?

The environment of 'masculinity' both served me well and caused me difficulty too. Materially it meant that I grew up with innate confidence and self-belief, a genuine conviction that I could do anything I turned my hand to. I expected to go to a good university. And I always knew, somehow, that I would land on my feet. I feel incredibly lucky to be able to say that.

The only difficulties I had were the privileged problems of, 'Am I doing enough with my life?', 'I can do anything, so it had better be good!' I put a lot of pressure on myself to be not just good enough but absolutely exceptional. It's a pressure I still carry in part, today, although one that's subsided over the years as I've explored my mental health in more depth.

Growing up, I remember every single year getting better and better, with more opportunities, friends, experiences, nights out; it was a dream and I was living it. Like many young people, university was an opportunity to find myself, try new things, wear new clothes, express myself differently – it was a time to experiment, without the burden of responsibility. However, the passions and interests I had carried at school or as a child had fizzled out. I went to university as a blank canvas, and rather than feeling excited by that, I felt scared. I began to ask the question, 'Who am I?'

I searched for my passions and what would define me. I felt drawn to the world of startups and entrepreneurship, after meeting my friend, and now co-founder, George, at university. The allure of entrepreneurship was so strong for me, it felt like the golden ticket to everything that I had ever wanted. I could be different and unique as an entrepreneur; I'd stand out and have the freedom to create my own life and working environment on my terms. And being a 'businessman' was something widely regarded as being successful, so I didn't feel like I was exposing too much of myself. The problem was, with hindsight, that all of my reasons for starting a business were quite shallow – they were just about me and my ego – I wanted a business to make me look good and to give me something to latch on to as an identity and a way to introduce myself.

I started a business at university with George and a couple of others, and we quickly fell down the rabbit hole into the world of startups. We raised investment, we built a small team, and for three and a half years we tried to create something out of nothing – and I really mean nothing because there was no deeper purpose, mission or problem-solving solution to drive the business. I was lost from the start, and for three years I ran on empty, trying to push myself further and further to make something happen, until I could push no more. I burned out, not because I had run out of fuel, but because I'd had none in the first place. My passion was never there, my intentions were never honest and, in the end, I pursued pushing on for the sake of pushing on.

This experience broke me, and the post-mortem on that first business was when mental health really came to the fore in my life. I'd spent three years sticking my chest out and wearing a mask in order to turn myself into something, to play a role and get ahead. I'd become fake in my professional life, where Monday to Friday was completely different from Friday to Sunday. For the entirety of running that first business I was insecure, scared, alone and anxious for the future, yet I pushed all those feelings down and did what I thought was required to tread the path to success. I persevered, faked it, 'blagged it', hustled and kept on keeping on. When that business was taken away, when my identity was reduced to just being James, I felt empty and incomplete, like I had a great hole in my chest. I was heartbroken and grieving, and I felt like a zero, a nobody.

Looking back, it's the most transformative place I've ever been, and I see now how touching rock bottom can be completely re-defining. Albeit, at the time, I didn't let on that I was deeply struggling. After I shut down the business and announced it as a failure, I felt like a complete failure myself. And yet I continued to put on an act and live my life in the same way. It was a mindless reality where I wasn't fully present; I wasn't honest enough to acknowledge my current feelings of sadness, anger and shame. I was numb.

In the end, I couldn't ignore the signs from my body. They were more like vibrations as I began feeling regularly anxious. What began as the Sunday-night blues and the Monday-morning dread became debilitating feelings of anxiety in my daily life. I began having panic attacks at work, in meetings, before meetings, and I would have to run to the bathroom to calm myself down before work. I was very fragile and felt exposed and raw.

This period of excruciating anxiety lasted about nine months, and I didn't let on to anyone at all for a long time; much of it I spent in my head, embarrassed that I was weak and annoyed that I was even feeling this way. I told myself that I was wrong to be in pain, that I shouldn't be feeling like this. I felt guilt for feeling bad because I didn't have problems big enough to feel bad about. In the end, no matter how many stories I told myself, or how much negative self-talk I tried to wrap myself in, I couldn't ignore the crippling anxiety.

From nowhere, I turned to a journal. I had no concept of journaling and picked it up on a night I can't even remember. I just began to write. I wrote and I wrote and I wrote. Initially, it was a way to diarize the events in my life that I knew would be quite memorable, yet it quickly become a cathartic outlet to share how I was feeling – a safe environment in which I could articulate my feelings. The journaling was profound because I put words to feelings and I slowly began to judge myself less. As I saw the plain reality of my words and my experiences on the page in front of me, they became more real and they became lighter too. I became kinder to myself for feeling the way I did.

I remember writing, 'I'm stressed and anxious,' and the relief I felt afterwards. I looked back at that sentence and it just clicked, in a moment of revelation, it felt so simple. I'm stressed and I'm anxious. Of course I am. From there my confidence began to grow and the process of opening up was under way. I was able to start putting words to my feelings, and I was able to separate myself from them and start to examine my emotions. I began to mention to friends that I wasn't feeling great, with varying degrees of success. Some friends were able to ask me lots of questions or soothe my anxiety, but sometimes I missed the mark and wasn't able to truly express how I was feeling.

These early experiences were part of me becoming aware of myself and my mental health for the first time ever. Truthfully, I wasn't changing much in my life at this point; the difficult part was that I was becoming more aware of just how unhappy I was. However, the suffering was halved by not judging myself for how I was feeling. Instead, I was allowing myself to feel it all and not numbing myself to the pain. This point in my life was evolutionary and a time of real change. There were many memorable experiences: conversations with close friends, moments of real sadness, moments of real anxiety. All the way from great conversations in the smoking area of a pub to standing in the toilet cubicle of a pub and thinking, 'I can't do this any more' (thoughts that would be silenced after three or four drinks). I had reached a crisis point that was very painful, but it would turn out to be completely transformational.

Eventually, I found the courage to write a public blog post about my experiences with mental health. At the time, I was very much running on instinct and I can't even really remember writing it. A voice within me was saying, 'You have to do this,' and so I did. I published an article called 'Mental Health in Startups' and my life changed at that point. I'd put my hands up publicly and said, 'This is me, this is who I am, and this is my story.'

My story really resonated with people and I got a deluge of responses from all walks of life. It was 2016 and mental health was just beginning to be talked about more in the public realm. Mine was one of those stories in the early stages of the movement. What I was saying was beginning to gain momentum. It was as if the world was inviting me to share my story, and I wasn't resisting. I felt exhilarated; for the first time in my life I was being completely, utterly me – baring the good and the bad – and people were not only accepting me, but thanking me for it. I was on an absolute high. I began to feel like I mattered again, like I belonged and like I was valuable. I was still healing and the storytelling was part of my healing. It was as if I was still journaling, just out loud; a lot of what I was saying was unfiltered and raw. I was being honest, not faking it, and sharing my story. I was being true.

I began to feel called to take a more active role. I knew I had to do something in mental health. I knew that people were crying out for something – for some support, for some change. I could feel the sense of momentum and revolution. Change was coming – in fact, it was already happening. It wasn't that the support wasn't out there, it was just that people felt like they couldn't access it – like they couldn't access mental health at all. From my pain and my attempts to address it, along with that insight, Sanctus was born. Initially, Sanctus was just the name for the movement; it was a brand to symbolize the mission to transform mental health and inspire people to view mental health like their physical health. I began shouting about a vision to put the world's first mental health gyms on the high street. I kept saying it, and saying it, and people's heads started turning as they began to take notice. I partnered with coaches and therapists to create group spaces, run events, host meet-ups, give talks and continue to tell my story, over and over again. I did whatever I could to create a community and bring the Sanctus mission to life.

Five years on, and I've dedicated much of my time and my energy to that mission, alongside building a sustainable approach to mental health in the workplace, with our early team and partners. We have played our part in shifting the perceptions of mental health. We've had a huge impact on mental health in the wider context, and specifically on mental health in the workplace. Through Sanctus we've worked with the best mental health advocates in the country, people who have introduced mental health into their workplaces and transformed their business culture.

I've seen that happen, and I've been grateful to have been part of their journey. We are very much still on that journey with them.

2 How to get the most from this book

Read it your way

I don't want this book to be another thing you 'should do'. There's no right way to read a book, and you don't have to read it in any particular order. Depending on your existing relationship with mental health, and your role at work too, certain chapters or sections in this book may not feel as relevant as others, so feel free to skip those or flick through. For example, if you are in a leadership position at your place of work, you may feel like you want to get to the actionable sections. On the other hand, if you are a mental health practitioner, the sections that focus on mental health specifically may feel familiar to you. Use this book in whatever way feels natural to you.

Share your journey

Please share this book too, and tell others you are reading it. That's not because I want others to buy it, but because I believe it'll enhance your experience to be sharing your mental health journey with others. Tell your colleagues you are reading this, tell your friends. That's the whole point of this – starting conversations on mental health – and you can do that right away.

My intention is to share experiences, learnings, insights and stories with you. It's then up to you to choose how and when you use them.

Take your time

You don't need to read this book by tomorrow. Try to slow down, go steady, listen, read, let the words sink in. We need an antidote to the always on, go-get- 'em world of work that most of us experience. By taking this slow, you'll feel more able to take it slow when you start having conversations about mental health at work. More able to listen, more able to be with people.

Take it slow while reading this book, support yourself throughout, set an intention for how you'd like to be: calm, still, focused, grounded. Complement picking up this book with other rituals in your life: making a hot drink, yoga to start the day, journaling, meditation, or whatever else works for you. Take it slow, don't rush, let yourself hear it. Go at your own pace because the intention here is to create something sustainable. We want long-term change around mental health in the workplace, and we can't do that if you're burned-out.

Notice what comes up

This book may make you feel a little uncomfortable at times, and that's completely okay. You may get a little hot under the collar. You may find yourself feeling sceptical or uninterested. You may find yourself feeling passionate, or enraged. You may find yourself feeling utterly relieved. You may find yourself feeling upset, emotional that finally someone 'gets' it. Whatever your response is, I hope there is one, and I hope you notice it, because that will mean you are connecting to the topic in some way – and that's a good thing.

This is about raising our awareness of mental health, developing our empathy and building our confidence in talking about it and making changes. We're not talking about how to assemble a washing machine, get more leads, grow your business, or 'how I did it'. This is about mental health at work, this is about happiness, fulfilment, health, well-being – and not just ours, but that of others too. This is about work, where we spend most of our time. This book is real, it's human, and I promise you its intention is to change something for the better. I don't know what your reason is for picking this book up – maybe you don't yet, either – but my guess is you want something to be different. You want something to change. You feel a flutter in your stomach, or a stirring in your heart. Or there's a quiet voice in your head whispering at night or screaming in the day. We're here to *make* a difference and to *feel* different – either for ourselves or for others. This book is for you, your boss, your colleagues, peers, family and friends – it's so we can change something at work that impacts everyone's mental health.

Start a journal

One practice I'd encourage you to pick up alongside this book is journaling: the consistent habit of writing down your thoughts, feelings and emotions. I invite you to start a journal and practise writing down the thoughts, feelings and emotions that are coming up for you along the way. Throughout the book you'll find reflective questions and prompts to get you started.

KEY POINTS

- You don't have to read this book in a weekend.
- Notice your responses throughout the book.
- Be patient, go slowly, be kind to yourself.
- Share that you're reading this book with someone.
- Create a habit or ritual for your mental health alongside reading.

Journaling questions

- What would you like to get out of reading this book? Set an intention.
- What would your dream mental health culture in the workplace be like? Imagine how things could be different to the way they are now.

Part 2 Mental Health

'What mental health needs is more sunlight, more candour, more unashamed conversation.'
Glenn Close

3 What is mental health?

If we are going to start to feel more comfortable talking about mental health at work, we need to understand the subject of mental health itself. There are decades of research and thousands of books and scholarly articles on mental health, psychotherapy and neuroscience that are in-depth and explore the mysteries and complexities of the human mind in rigorous detail. My intention isn't to do that here: my aim is to start a discussion around mental health and make it easy to understand, comfortable to play with and not as scary as I've probably already made it sound by using the words 'neuroscience' and 'psychotherapy'.

Part of the fear surrounding mental health is fear of the unknown. What will happen if you start talking about your mental health or someone else's? And then there's the unknown of mental health itself.

- How does my mind work?
- Why do I feel tight in my chest when I'm anxious?
- Why can't I get myself out of bed when I have a certain meeting at work?
- Why do I feel the way I do when I can see no obvious reason at all?

The variables, the complexity, the hard truths of mental health, these are all incredibly difficult to look at, and most of us have received very little education about mental health at all. We have minimal understanding of the human body and our physical health. We may know that the femur is the longest bone in the body. We may know that for a headache or cold we should take paracetamol or ibuprofen, drink lots of water and get plenty of rest. This is because most of us were taught the basics about physical health at school. What we weren't taught was to notice how we're feeling. We weren't taught about anger, sadness, anxiety, stress or suicide.

Growing up, few of us are given the options or resources to learn about our mental health, whether during our education or from family, friends or wider society. We are approaching this subject with very limited taught or acquired knowledge. Instead, what most of us are left with is no defined understanding of how to discuss mental health in our lives. Combine that with our own trauma or challenging life experiences and we're left with a pretty shambolic concoction. It's unsurprising that so many people are completely illiterate about their mental health, and that's why so many people are left suffering in silence.

Viewed through this lens, the way we are currently approaching mental health in our society is stuck in the dark ages. The modern world becomes ever more complex and interconnected, with more threats to our mental health. And yet, most of us currently receive no education about our mental health, our emotions and our feelings, and how to cope and thrive in today's world. We have the opportunity to change that for ourselves and to pave the way for future generations. I believe it's not only desperately needed, but a moral responsibility for us too.

How do we define mental health?

I invite you now to think about your own definition of mental health. What is mental health to you? What comes up when you think about mental health? You may think of images of asylums, you may think about tears and sadness, or stress and anxiety. The first images that come to my mind are talking and people coming together to talk, but yours will be influenced by your own experiences.

Rather than giving you a comprehensive and fixed definition of what mental health is, this book will focus on the process of how we get there and how we have the conversation. For example, if you read on and feel that what I'm saying is incorrect, and you have a strong negative reaction to it, which you then talk about with a friend or someone in your life, I see that as a huge win. I want us to define mental health together, by engaging in a dialogue between us, rather than me just stating my viewpoint and holding that up as true for everyone; when we see things together, perhaps we may see them a little differently. By holding up different viewpoints, and different ways of looking at things, we'll create more room for diversity, connection and conversation – all of which are good for mental health.

I invite you to expand your own view of mental health by making an attempt to really listen to someone else's viewpoint. Depending on our upbringing and cultural references, mental health will hold wildly different meanings for many of us.

Mental health is not an idealized emotional state

Good or positive mental health is not feeling happy all the time, or being a certain way all the time. This is one of the biggest traps I have continued to fall into; the idea that we all have to find 'perfect' mental health. I used to think that not being angry was good mental health, that not being sad and always being positive or framing things in an upbeat way was good mental health. It has been a huge learning experience for me to slowly detach myself from labelling certain emotions as 'good' or 'bad', 'positive' or 'negative', and to just let them be. For a long time, I saw anger as a really bad emotion, not to be allowed into my life or relationships, so instead I would push it down and repress it. However, this act of suppressing my anger was bad for my mental health because I was repressing my emotion, and spending energy on having to 'pretend' because of the label and judgement I was giving to a particular emotion.

Much of the stigma in mental health comes from the fact that we view certain emotions (or emotions at all in some cases) as good or bad. Yet, if we see emotions simply as information coming from our body, then we can look at mental health more simply as the way our mind functions, rather than labelling the end result.

Mental health isn't an end goal

When we use a physical health analogy, we have been sold a set of goals over the years. A six-pack, or single-digit percentage body fat, or the ability to touch our toes, or to run a 10k in fifty minutes. It's easy to believe that this approach works for mental health too. Always be happy, outgoing, positive all the time, meditating every morning, always calm, and completely, totally, always compassionate. But these goals can be unattainable. In fact, the pursuit of this state of perfection can inadvertently be another way to be hard on ourselves, to judge ourselves and tell ourselves we're not good enough.

Mental health is a process

If we look at mental health as a process, a way of being and functioning, then we start to look at our actions and our behaviours with curiosity rather than judgement.

This view of mental health stems from a particular view of the mind. When we say, 'We all have mental health,' what we are saying is that we all have a mind. The mind emerges from our body and our nervous system as a way of us processing and regulating the flow of energy and information that is constantly around us. It is our mind that is taking information from our environment, from the people around us, from our past experiences, via our nervous system and our body. Our mind itself is a constant process that isn't fixed or defined; it is constantly moving, constantly in flux. Our mind is there to regulate our responses while being in contact with the world around us. Which means our thoughts, our feelings, our emotions do not arise out of nowhere, they are our response, our reaction, and they are part of our process. Thus we're not 'crazy' when we feel something strongly, or when we feel sick to the stomach before public speaking.

We are part of something bigger than just 'I'

A dominant view of mental health has been to see it as something that is broken and needs fixing. This plays to a very individualistic view of mental health, which has led us to believe that how we feel is completely limited to how we are on the inside, without taking into consideration our environmental situation, our relationships and the global connected system within which we operate. When we view the mind as a process, and our mental health as the health of that process, then we see that we are not just a cog functioning alone, we are part of a much wider and more complex environment. We are part of the world, an ecosystem, a community. We are constantly in touch with the world, with different experiences, people and places, all of which will impact our mind and our mental health all the time.

Make room for curiosity

This view of mental health enables us to look deeper and to inquire, as opposed to judging the end result. The lack of a defined right or wrong gives us permission to speak openly from the heart about our experiences, knowing that there's a reason for those experiences and how we are relating to the world.

You may feel deeply connected to what I am writing, or you may have a humungous frown across your forehead. I don't believe it is possible for me to write a description of mental health that is going to resonate with and relate to everyone. How you are responding to this right now is not 'right' or 'wrong', it is simply your response. I invite you to be curious about your response and to question why you may be feeling connected, inspired, confused or frustrated. I invite you to go further than this book in your listening, reading and understanding too. It's unlikely you'll want to read a textbook on psychotherapy or mental health, so watch videos, read blog posts, listen to podcasts and read how-to books.

You may have questions about what you've read so far.

- 'Okay, if the mind is a process, if mental health is a way of functioning, what is a good process?'
- 'How do I regulate myself?'
- 'How do I feel less stuck and trapped?'

Some of these questions may feel urgent for you – they may even have an exclamation mark at the end! However, I ask you to slow down and remember that this book is about starting a process. I believe that the best way to define mental health for yourself is to *define it for yourself*. I invite you to begin, now.

Start looking at your mental health, questioning, reaching out and exploring.

Start with you.

KEY POINTS

- 'Good' mental health is not an idealized emotional state, such as being happy.
- You already have your own perception of and relationship to mental health.
- We need to initiate a dialogue about mental health together.

- We must inquire into our own mental health to define it.
- Notice how you are responding to this chapter.

Journaling questions

- What does mental health mean to you?
- What have been your experiences with mental health?

4 Mental health myths

Mental health is misunderstood. Many of us are both ill-informed and highly sensitive about the subject – a dangerous cocktail. We all have an opinion on mental health, and we all have life experiences that define our opinions. Those experiences are powerful, and yet we may be unaware of their influence. It's important to be aware of the common myths and misconceptions that may have informed our view of mental health, and the view of others too.

Our cultural understanding of mental health is stuck in the twentieth century. The world has changed, we have evolved, and our understanding of mental health has to move with the times. We can't move forward with our own mental health, or with mental health at work, if our own view of mental health is still characterized by outdated slogans and cultural norms. It's important to recognize the myths that are alive in our offices and workplaces. It's our job to understand them and then bust them.

'I don't have mental health'

This myth is simple and dangerously effective. It touches on the deeply held belief that mental health *isn't* something that we all have. That, in fact, it's something that others have, and when those others 'have mental health' we pity them and we feel sorry for them. It shows up in misplaced language that I encourage you to start looking out for, phrases such as, 'I've been fortunate enough never to have had mental health.'

As a society we talk about mental health as if it's a foreign body that invades the minds of certain people at whim. We take little ownership of mental health, and many of us don't yet feel connected to our own concept of mental health, or even know how to put it into words.

On a deeper level, there's a systemic belief that mental health represents only mental 'ill-health'. That mental health encapsulates only mental 'illness' and only mental health 'issues'. Mental health is something we all have and need to pay attention to.

'Others have it worse than me'

This statement will almost always be true. If we all lived by this and used it as an excuse not to talk about how we feel, not to share our suffering or ask for help, then nobody would ever get any help – and nobody would talk about their mental health, ever. There will always be people who are in a worse situation than you. That's not a reason not to share your own experience or to get the help you need, but it's often an excuse or an avoidance tactic.

One of the great mental health misconceptions is that our problems aren't 'enough'. That what is going on in our lives isn't good enough, big enough or bad enough to talk about because others are worse off, and so we should be grateful. It's a problem of privilege. The fact that you are reading this book means that, like me, you have probably lived a fairly privileged life on a global spectrum. Yet that does not mean that we don't all deserve the space, time and opportunity to share how we are feeling, however major or minor that may seem when compared to the life experiences of others.

It's all relative – what is a huge thing for one person may feel like a small thing to someone else. It's not about the content of the problem; it's the context and severity of your response that matters. One person may be deeply depressed and feel unable to get out of bed for weeks on end. Another person may feel dissatisfied with their well-paid job at a good company. Yet another person may feel frustrated every time their boss makes a certain comment. Every example is worthy of being listened to, every person is worthy of being seen and heard by someone. Every example is impacting someone's mental health in some way.

When we open our eyes and see that we all have mental health, all of the time, then we expand our range of what is 'worth talking about' and what is 'enough'. There's no right, wrong, good, bad, better or worse – it's all true at the same time. Someone can be suffering deeply and having suicidal thoughts, and someone else can want a better job or a promotion – neither is better or worse than the other – they are both deeply human experiences and represent two ends of a long and winding mental health continuum.

'Mental health is weakness'

Some people confuse mental health with weakness, seeing it as a negative reflection of your character or ability. Unfortunately, this mantra rules in many workplaces. Any form of vulnerability is shut down or hidden away because to show any sense of your human fallibility, vulnerability or insecurity may be preyed upon as a sign of weakness. This cultural norm is what frequently shuts down the conversation on mental health at work – in fact, worse, it doesn't even let it begin. It creates a barren landscape where no emotions can grow, other than the well-accepted (often masculine) emotions or ways of showing up. Anything else isn't just frowned upon, it is judged and labelled as 'worse'.

The good news is this myth isn't just being busted, it is changing for the better. Vulnerability is strength, not weakness. Being able to ask for help is strength, not weakness. Talking about your mental health is strength, not weakness. It takes courage to talk about your mental health. It takes self-awareness to ask for help. It takes bravery to bring mental health into the workplace.

Talking about mental health at all, in any context, takes strength. This perception of vulnerability – this reluctance to talk about our feelings and mental health more generally – is what is currently being transformed in our world.

In conclusion

> We all have mental health.

There are many myths, stories and misconceptions that we have about our mental health. I've named three that I believe to be the most pervasive across our society. There are many more, and we'll all have our own stories that we tell ourselves, based on our role, family circumstances, heritage, tradition, gender and more. I invite you to think about what stories you may be telling yourself when it comes to mental health. Here are just a few that I've encountered.

- 'Talking about your feelings is always painful.'
- 'Sometimes people share too much.'
- 'Some stuff just shouldn't be talked about.'

Write down the stories that resonate with you, then take a look at those stories and see what you can learn from them.

KEY POINTS

- We all have mental health.
- Everyone's experiences with mental health are valid and deserve to be heard.
- Mental health is not weakness.

Journaling questions

- What stories do you tell yourself about mental health?
- How have you responded when you've heard others share their stories or experiences of mental health?
- What parts of mental health are you sceptical about?

5 Boundaries

Spend five minutes with a coach or therapist, or a bit of time reading self-care blogs, and I promise you the word 'boundaries' will come up. Before I started getting into mental health, I thought boundaries were just something in cricket – and that's it. As it turns out, the boundary in cricket is quite a helpful place for us to start thinking about boundaries in a wider sense. On a cricket pitch the boundary is the big piece of rope that marks the outer limits of the field of play, and there are certain rules around what happens when a person (or ball) is inside or outside the boundary. It's not so different from our own boundaries.

Why we need boundaries

We all have our individual boundaries when it comes to mental health, in terms of what we feel able to do and not to do, what we feel able to say and not to say, what role we feel able to play, and where we do or don't feel comfortable. We even have boundaries around what topics we feel comfortable discussing with people. At work, some simple examples may be boundaries around our working hours, or what tasks we say yes and no to, with regards to our role. Our boundaries are shaped by many things: our values; our skillset and knowledge; our sense of what's important to us. In my experience, many people who are employed or find themselves in a helping or caring position really struggle with their boundaries – and in particular, they struggle to say no. In general, we all struggle to say no in our personal lives – I know I certainly have done. Holding a boundary is hard.

Boundaries are there to protect us, and to protect others too. Having a clear sense of boundaries when it comes to mental health creates safety and protects people from emotional harm and potentially traumatic interactions.

Boundaries in mental health advocacy

In this book I have been clear from the start that I am not a mental health practitioner trained in a methodology of how to lead people towards healing or growth in their lives. I am a mental health advocate, passionate about the topic, guided by my lived experience. If I began offering you personal advice or guidance about your mental health, then that would be stepping outside what I feel comfortable with. I'd be well outside my boundaries and I wouldn't be acting in line with what I believe is safe and ethical.

There will be some of you reading this book who have gained particular skills or qualifications, perhaps in coaching, counselling, therapy or psychology, and you may feel equipped to advise and support individuals around mental health. However, as a mental health advocate, I am not a practitioner. My job is not to work with 'clients' to support their mental health but to champion mental health, so we can all talk about it more openly and productively. Of course, if that does support people's growth and healing, that's a brilliant outcome, but I don't want to do that work on a one-to-one basis.

Know your own boundaries

If you are reading this book as someone with few or no mental health qualifications or direct skills, just be yourself and recognize your boundaries for what they are. Do not pretend or try to be anything other than the person you are. If you are in HR, you are in HR. If you are a manager, you are a manager. If you are a CEO, be a CEO. There is no need to step outside your comfort zone, venturing into a different realm and pretending to be something you are not. This is potentially dangerous for you and others, it's emotionally exhausting, and it may not support people in the best possible way. Put simply, you are your role within your workplace and you are a human being.

Your role is not to give mental health advice to others. It is not to support people in directly exploring or deepening their experience of their mental health. Your role is not to be someone's counsellor, therapist or coach. Your role is not to have people rely on you for their mental health. There is a lot you don't know about mental health, and you have not been trained in this field. You have your own experiences of mental health, and your journey is only just starting, so you cannot step outside your boundaries safely, you can only go to the edges of the area that you have defined for yourself. This doesn't mean that you cannot talk about mental health – if it did, then this book would serve little purpose. It means that you can safely and adequately have certain types of conversations about mental health, and you can talk about mental health in a defined way. The aim of this book is to support you in talking more about mental health, but in a way that feels right and is within your boundaries. I believe that by being clear on your boundaries, you'll be able to have more conversations about mental health – and you'll feel good about it. You won't feel scared, or feel like you're doing something wrong, because you'll have a clear understanding of your role, and you won't get yourself into potentially weird or uncomfortable situations where you have crossed a boundary into something murky and unknown.

Don't be afraid to be yourself

In the next chapter we're going to look at having conversations about mental health, and boundaries will come up again. For now, this is key: do not try to be anything more than you are when talking about mental health. If you're a manager or in HR, I appreciate the boundaries can start to feel a little blurry, and yet if you play your role, staying within the boundaries of that role, it doesn't mean you can't be human too.

Being a mental health advocate means sharing your story, exploring your own mental health, talking about your experience and listening deeply to the experiences of others. Anybody can do that, without crossing any lines. You can talk about how you've had a similar experience before – or how you never have, so you can't imagine it. You can say how you feel out of your depth in this conversation, how you feel like you're past the point where you have been with your mental health. You can say that you don't think your workplace has loads on offer, but together you can work out what you can do. As a manager you can even hold someone accountable for doing something about their mental health, if it's in line with their role and has come up in the conversation.

There's a lot you can do for mental health that sits safely within your boundaries as an individual at work. You can meet someone, connect with them, hear them and let others know that they have been seen by you, that they matter and that you care. You can do all of that without taking on a lot of emotional baggage, and without expending loads of energy. You can simply be yourself and truly be with others.

Bring mental health into your relationships, into your work, and that alone as your gift to the world will be enough.

KEY POINTS

- Be aware when you feel like you are stepping outside your comfort zone in relationships.
- You are not a coach, therapist or counsellor (unless you've been trained).
- Listening, connecting and communicating about mental health is part of being human and can be done safely within your boundaries.

Journaling questions

- When have you felt like you've been pushed outside of your boundaries?
- What role can you play in the mental health at work movement?

6 Risk

We need to talk about the elephant in the room: suicide. At the most basic level, many people are afraid to talk about mental health in case their actions or words lead somebody to take their own life, or harm themselves or others. They may be scared to explore their own mental health for fear of where that path may lead them. Suicide is a very real risk, as are other forms of dangerous activity with regards to mental health. People may become a danger to themselves or others, and may harm themselves or other people. And yet, by not talking about it, we're making it something taboo and scary. The truth is, it is very possible that someone you know, at home or at work, is struggling with their mental health right now. There's no point hiding from this sad truth – in fact, by hiding from it, we're creating more shame and making it harder for people who are really suffering to get the potentially life-changing support they may need.

Talking about it doesn't make it happen

People do not take their own life because there's been a conversation about mental health, or because someone talked about it and it made them feel worse. In fact, by not opening the subject up, people may feel like they've not been listened to, their fears have been dismissed, or that nobody cares about them.

Talking about mental health at work may bring up more issues and raise awareness, yet it won't make things worse than they are; it'll just highlight what was already there in the first place. We need to be more confident in talking about suicide because it's increasingly important to do so. By speaking plainly and openly about all aspects of mental health, including suicide, we remove the shame and the stigma around it. When it comes to suicide, doing this can save someone's life. There are plenty of incredible training resources out there that will help you to initiate conversations with people about suicide, and I encourage you to explore them. My task here is to break down the stigma that surrounds mental health, and to include suicide within that too.

Letting in the light

As you open up your own dialogue around mental health you'll start to draw back the curtain and you'll see more clearly, illuminating issues both in your own life and in your workplace. That's the beauty of mental health; it enlightens the richness, diversity and complexity of our lives and reinforces our humanity in a way that feels real and alive. It can be scary too. The uncertainty of what we may find can be frightening, especially if we sense that we may uncover something that we've been hiding away from. It's this fear, whether conscious or unconscious, that often stops many people from openly exploring their mental health; it's the fear of what may be lurking in the unknown.

This is true on an individual level in all of our own personal mental health journeys, and it's also true for a workplace environment as a collective. We're scared to uncover that John in Sales doesn't actually want to be here, and wants to leave because he isn't passionate about what we do. Or that the CEO actually just cares about making money and is very resistant to change. Or that Sally in Marketing is pushing people away and won't let anyone help her. Who knows what we might uncover by opening the door to mental health and the myriad of emotions it brings up? And if we uncover it and see it, we can't unsee it, we'll have to do something about it.

This is a choice you make in your life, both inside and outside work. It's about choosing a different way of being, one that is conscious, open-hearted and real. It's hard because the world can go from black and white to colour, from standard definition to HD. You are deciding whether to tread this path and be open to the possibilities it will throw up for you. You have picked this book up for a reason, though, and I imagine that, on some level, you want something different for yourself and for your work. Perhaps a world where we don't turn off our humanity to go to work, where we can be truly ourselves when we are at work, where our emotions are allowed, permitted – and not just the ones people like, but perhaps the more difficult ones too. That means that we open ourselves up to difficult emotions and the reality of when we, and others, are struggling.

Creating a new kind of risk

It is beyond doubt that we will all struggle with our mental health at certain points in our lives. As you open up the conversation on mental health at work, by giving permission and space for people to share how they might be feeling more openly, you create a different kind of risk at work. Before, the risk was that someone would leave your business because they were unhappy, but you couldn't put your finger on why. Or someone would be signed off sick, and you didn't quite understand why it was happening so frequently. Or someone at work would take their own life, and you'd have absolutely no idea why (other than the stories you might make up in your head). As your conversations around mental health become more mature, and everyone becomes more literate and open-minded in their responses to mental health, the same risks apply. Yet the difference is that you may know why, you may understand – and actually, that may feel more painful for you and others in the team.

The risks within mental health are risks that we all face in our lives. None of us is immune to feeling depressed, anxious or suicidal. We can work on our mental health, we can heal what we may have experienced in the past, we can prioritize our self-care, yet we are still likely to experience mental health issues at some point in our life. If we accept this view and open our eyes to the reality that we all have mental health, and we are all human, then I believe we have a moral obligation and a human duty to focus on our mental health, at work and beyond. Forget the commercial impacts of employer brand, employee attrition rates and think only about the human impact on health, well-being and relationships, and that is enough to bring mental health to the forefront.

Recognizing the potential benefits

What we will see as we explore the rest of this book, and hear stories from leaders and businesses, is the potential upside of creating an environment of open discussion around mental health.

The benefits – for employers, companies and individuals – are limitless. While the risks are known and are very clear, we've barely even got started yet on what the opportunities are – for everyone who is involved.

Talking about mental health at work is a huge opportunity for us all to grow and to reach new potential. There are downsides that we must minimize and protect against, yet there are huge upsides too.

KEY POINTS

- By avoiding talking about suicide we create more shame around it.
- Talking about suicide and/or mental health does not encourage or increase the potential for harmful behaviour.
- By accepting the risks of mental health, we create the possibility for the positives and benefits too.

Journaling questions

- When it comes to mental health, what are you afraid of?
- What can you feel in your body when you're reading this section?
- What opportunities do you see for mental health at work?

Part 3 Your Story

'Courage starts with showing up and letting ourselves be seen.'
Brené Brown

7 Start with you

> Put on your own oxygen mask before helping others.

It's time to do some work. The good news is it's easy to get started and anyone can do it. You can start in whatever way you want, and there is no way to get it wrong. You don't have to turn into Sigmund Freud or Brené Brown overnight. You don't have to be able to meditate on one leg for forty-two days straight or catch a fly with chopsticks. This isn't about you becoming an expert, it's about you becoming an advocate by looking at your own mental health first, before anything else. You can only play your part in the mental health movement if you first do the work yourself, on yourself. You have to talk the talk and walk the walk. It's just that, in this case, the walking *is* the talking. Anyone can bring the mental health conversation into the workplace – and that means you. Even if you're not the CEO or on the leadership team and don't have budget responsibility, you can be an instigator, a fire starter. You can get the mental health agenda moving at work by participating in it.

There's a reason why you are reading about mental health at work. You may want work to be different, or you may want to feel different at work. Follow your desire into mental health, and through doing that you'll have a positive impact on others along the way.

The best way to be part of the mental-health-at-work revolution is to start your own mental health journey. Here's why.

1. By practising, playing and working on your own mental health, you'll be able to talk about mental health more confidently, drawing on your own experiences.
2. You'll naturally develop more empathy for others and increase your knowledge of issues surrounding mental health as you expand what you know about yourself.
3. You'll have experiences to share with others that create permission to speak, ensure safety, and inspire curiosity and conversation.
4. You'll come across more authentically when talking about mental health to others at work.
5. Your mental health *is* you, so whatever your experiences are, you'll carry them with you, in your personal life and also in the workplace.

Trust your intuition

Everyone is different, and what people feel drawn to is incredibly diverse. Anything can be good for your mental health, from exercise, to reading, to films, to music, to travelling, to wild swimming, to yoga and so much more. You will know what you feel drawn to; it may have been this book, but it could also be yoga, therapy, coaching, meditation or journaling. Try making a list of things that you'd like to give a go. Whatever you decide to do, I encourage you to get started.

By prioritizing your own mental health you will be a role model in your company, encouraging your colleagues to do the same. You'll build the credibility and integrity to be a powerful advocate for mental health at work. There may be a conversation about mental health that you feel most drawn to, perhaps with someone in your life, or even someone at work. Work can be a safe space to have discussions with peers about mental health, especially if your family situation doesn't feel like a safe place to begin talking about it. Begin your mental health journey by trying new things, new ways of looking after yourself, or new experiences in which you feel like you are growing.

You can't authentically be part of change around mental health at work without talking openly about mental health and, of course, it's going to be more compelling if your reason for doing it is connected to your own personal experiences. However, that doesn't make it any easier, and your heart will likely be saying, 'I'm scared to do this,' or, 'I don't know where to start.' You may be thinking that you don't even know what to say. Just as with mental health in general, there are a lot of misconceptions about how it will feel when you talk about your mental health for the first time, or when you try something new that's linked to your mental health in some way.

Choose how much to share

People often think they have to share absolutely everything; people think that when they start talking they just won't be able to stop and it'll all come pouring out. None of that is true. You are in control of what you share, and you can always choose how much you share, with whom, or what practices you pick up in your life. This isn't about pushing you to radically change your life right now and share everything with everyone. However, you can get started in ways that feel easy and aren't overwhelming. Your first conversation about mental health at work doesn't have to be you sharing your life story. It could be as simple as one sentence, it could be a question, it could just be saying the words 'mental health' in a meeting. Your first step in bringing mental health into your working life can be a small, small step – you can just inch forward. Have the courage to ask a question, make small talk, or share some of your experience.

Support yourself to speak up

I remember the first time I talked about mental health in a work setting; I had a panic attack in the toilet before I did it. It was a monthly team catch-up with my two managers, who were the owners of the business, and I was nervous. I was nervous to even say the phrase 'mental health'. I thought they were going to tell me I was stupid, or that it wasn't something I should be spending my time on. In the end, I didn't say much.

At the end of the meeting I just said, 'I'm spending a bit of time looking into mental health as it's something I'm interested in.' That was it, that was the start.

And my big show-stopping sentence was met with, 'Okay.' That's all.

On reflection, I wasn't supporting myself enough and even speaking up in that meeting felt like too big a step; I certainly wasn't taking my own advice about getting started with my own mental health. In hindsight, I should have started to look at ways to support myself first, and then I'd have felt more able to go into that meeting without having a panic attack in the toilet beforehand. Wherever you start, you have to feel comfortable about going there, and it's got to feel like you're pushing at your boundaries but you're not in panic mode. I remember getting started with journaling, meditation and yoga and I found them difficult because I'd never experienced anything like them before, yet they were where I felt like I could start. I remember, too, quitting drinking for a while and going out less, doing Dry January and telling my friends and work colleagues about it and why I was doing it. Diving into therapy – or anything more intimate like that – would have felt like a big risk and one I wasn't ready for.

In the end, it was those practices that started to change how I felt, and then I started to have small, light-touch interactions around mental health in my working life. The things I started doing for myself were enough for me to bring mental health into the conversation, even if, looking back, they were small things.

Find a safe place to start

Who you end up chatting to about this stuff won't necessarily be who you are closest to at work or in the company; it doesn't have to be your boss or even your direct team. It just has to be whoever you feel safe enough to have the chat with. It could be someone in another department who you have a connection with, it could be someone in HR, someone in your team, it could be your manager – because you have a great relationship. Who knows? My sense is that you will already know someone you could start this conversation with.

If you feel like the best place to start for you is to share your own experience, then you have to feel safe with the other person to do this. This can be the most impactful way to start, as any expression of vulnerability breeds trust and intimacy. Starting is definitely the hardest part, and those first conversations – however surface level, or however 'deep' they may feel – can be tricky and nerve-racking. It's complex because you need to feel an element of safety to even bring up the notion of mental health, and yet by doing so you are creating greater safety around the issue too. You may mention mental health in a team meeting, and see someone else's eyes light up because you have just created permission for them to talk about it.

However you decide to take that first managed risk, you're going to create more permission and more safety for others when they feel ready to talk about mental health. Soon it won't just be you doing this; you won't feel alone, as you'll start to find your tribe. Whether you're ready to share your experience of how you're feeling right now, or whether you prefer to wait and do it in the future, a conversation like this at work can be incredibly impactful for you and for others too. Having safe and effective conversations about mental health can be transformative and deeply rewarding. This is how our culture around mental health is going to actually change: by talking to each other, meeting each other and actually connecting with each another. The future here is intimate workplace relationships based on trust and deep connections.

No one is too small to make a difference

You can impact mental health in your workplace. Whoever you are at work. I have seen it to be true. It's easy to feel powerless at work, to believe you can't have an impact outside your role, or even within it. You may feel helpless too, as if you are the victim of a culture that you have no way of influencing.

It's true that in certain roles it's harder to affect mental health at work. If you're in HR, then you have a real chance of bringing about change. If you're on the leadership team, you have a seat at the table. If you are the founder or a CEO, you're in charge so it's within your power. But I have seen many people in diverse roles, at all levels, with various types of experience, make a difference to mental health at their place of work through sheer passion and determination.

I believe it is possible to make a difference to your mental health culture, no matter what role you are in, just by following your own interest in mental health. This is why it has to start with you; you have the power.

CASE STUDIES

Hannah's story

I met Hannah Millard at Just Eat. She joined the company at twenty-three, as a Recruitment Co-ordinator, and through a mixture of luck and desire ended up taking on mental health as a project under the diversity and well-being remit. Hannah had experienced some tough times with her own mental health at university. She'd never quite figured things out, they just kind of subsided, so when she moved to Just Eat she still had a personal desire to understand more about her own mental health, while also believing that if she'd had these kinds of experiences with her own mental health, others would have too. Hannah's initiative to take on mental health at work wasn't purely selfish, yet she wanted to know more, for herself.

She wanted to create a more open culture, for herself. She wanted to bring in more support, for herself. But she wanted to do all this for others too.

In her time at Just Eat, Hannah ended up leading the change in mental health culture. Alongside the introduction of comprehensive individual support from a free mindfulness platform accessible to everyone, the company introduced mental health coaching on-site for all employees too. They won awards, received heartfelt messages from staff, saw senior leaders talk openly about mental health, and Hannah left a legacy of transformation around mental health. Hannah's is a success story and she's living proof that anyone can make a difference to mental health at work, whatever their level. Hannah's journey started with a personal story, a personal connection, which provided the fuel for her journey. Hannah began by having conversations with her manager, talking about her experiences. She asked to work on mental health in the workplace, and even though she started off in recruitment she ended up leading on mental health across the entire business.

It takes bravery and courage to be public about your mental health at work, and not everyone will want to do that. However, if you make your passion and interest known and available, then opportunities will arise; chances that you may not have been aware of will present themselves. This is what happened to Hannah at Just Eat. If she had kept her interest in mental health quiet, if she had ignored her own calling to focus on her own mental health, then who knows what might have happened? Maybe she would never have looked at mental health, and maybe Just Eat wouldn't have the wonderful mental health offerings that it now has. Hannah didn't hit a ceiling; her passionate interest in mental health at work was nurtured, was championed, and she was allowed to pursue it. This luxury may not be afforded to everyone in their workplace. It wasn't Hannah alone who transformed Just Eat's approach to mental health; there were supportive managers and an available budget. There must be Hannahs in every workplace, who speak up and pursue their passion in mental health, and there must be the desire to hear those voices too. At Just Eat, there were both.

You don't have to be the CEO to make a difference. You can be the person who starts the ball rolling and gets a topic on the CEO's desk. You can be the person who says yes to a mental health project at work. You can be the person who participates in the mental health event that one of your colleagues has worked so hard to create. Activism in mental health at work can happen in many different ways, from the top down and from the ground up. It's up to you to decide how you participate. Getting started with your own experience is how you or anyone can contribute.

KEY POINTS

- You can't be a mental health advocate without getting started with your own mental health.
- You intuitively know where you feel comfortable starting.
- You don't have to share your life story with anyone.
- Start small.

Journaling questions

- What practices or exercises for mental health do you feel drawn to?
- Where would be a good place for you to get started with your mental health?

8 How to talk to someone about your mental health

> The hardest part is getting started. Just start.

Talking about mental health at work is hard. If you're the CEO it'll feel scary because you'll fear judgement. If you're not the CEO, you'll still fear judgement. Talking about mental health can be hard, for everyone. But there could be a number of reasons why you want to deepen the conversation around mental health with someone at work.

- You may be experiencing some difficult emotions that are impacting your work.
- You may be experiencing something in your private life that is impacting your ability to work.
- You may feel unsupported at work and want to say it.
- You may see mental health as a development or growth opportunity for you and want to find out more.

Whatever depth you want to go into in a conversation about

mental health, you'll want to feel safe doing so and trust that you're entering into a conversation where you won't be judged. You'll also need to know that there won't be negative repercussions to what you want to share. Here's how to approach the conversation.

Become aware of the fear

A good place to start is to reflect on what you are afraid of and to vocalize your fears. You may not feel able to talk about mental health at work, for a variety of reasons:

- feeling like you'll be dismissed or judged
- feeling like you'll be held back at work in future
- being fearful that you'll share too much or you'll expose yourself more than you want to (for example, by crying).

We must ask ourselves, 'What is holding me back from having this conversation?' or, 'What am I afraid of?' As we vocalize our fear, it can be easier to see things a little more clearly.

Practise with people first

You can practise vocalizing these fears with friends, peers, family or other colleagues first, which can help you feel heard and start to articulate your feelings better. It's important to practise conversations around mental health with people you feel safe with in your life, or to find safe spaces to do that. Those safe spaces could mean contacting therapists, counsellors or helplines.

Another helpful reflection might be: what's happened in the past at work, or elsewhere, that makes it feel difficult to talk about your mental health? Or what's made it feel easy? Again, the responses here can be the perfect segues into meaningful conversations with people, before having the important conversation at work.

Be clear about what you want

Before taking the conversation further, you need to know what you want to get from the conversation. Ask yourself the following questions:

- Do you want to be heard?
- Do you want something to change?

It's your responsibility when talking about your own mental health to reflect on your experience and fears and move towards a clearer understanding of what you need. Then don't be afraid to ask for it.

Create the right environment

Picking the right environment to have the conversation is important. Whether at home or in the office, a level of discretion and confidentiality for any conversation around mental health is key, no matter the degree of vulnerability. It creates safety and allows for an honest conversation.

Find a space in which you feel comfortable to have the conversation.

Manage your expectations

Mental health holds a lot of emotion for all of us. We never have any idea what other people are experiencing until they tell us. The person you want to talk to may be feeling exactly the same, or mental health may have had a huge impact on their life, or they may not be in touch with their mental health at all.

It's important to remember that you may not get what you want from a conversation around mental health at work. You may have to change something, or find support elsewhere.

Remember, everyone has a story and we don't always get the connection we may be looking for.

Realize the power of sharing your story

We all have a responsibility when it comes to mental health at work. While people in leadership positions have the power to make decisions and the power to make changes, it doesn't mean that responsibility around mental health lies solely at a leadership level. Everyone has a responsibility for their own mental health. If you are deeply dissatisfied with your work and it is impacting your mental health negatively, then it is your responsibility to take ownership of your own life and begin to face that. The leadership team in any business are not responsible for the feelings of employees, they are responsible for the workplace environment they create. How people respond to that is personal to them. This comes up when people ask, 'Whose responsibility is mental health at work?' It's everyone's responsibility, not just the CEO's, or HR's. Our mental health is our responsibility, and everyone must take ownership of their own feelings and responses to the workplace environment.

There's a lot of blame and shame when it comes to mental health at work, and we are working within a global environment that is littered with distrust. There is widespread distrust in brands, leaders and politicians, and this spreads into the workplace. I hear childish blame that goes both ways: 'They just don't get it,' or, 'They expect too much.' The leadership dynamic in a lot of businesses echoes a parent–child relationship, except that everyone in the workplace is an adult. At work everyone has a responsibility to be an adult and notice their own tendencies to blame others or act as a victim when it's 'someone else's fault'. Work is a relationship, a contract between us, and we are all complicit in our actions within that. That's why everyone must tackle mental health in the workplace, not just sit back and wait for someone else to fix it.

Work influences everyone's mental health, and it's our personal responsibility to be accountable for our part in that. Our role will often be in line with our role in the workplace system. If you are in a management or pastoral role in a company, your remit is to listen and to share your own story too. If you have no management responsibilities, you still need to listen and open your eyes to what is going on around you; you have a responsibility to share how work is impacting you and to be open and honest about your experiences within the workplace environment.

If no one speaks up and no one listens, then stories around mental health do not enter the workplace culture. If stories and experiences around mental health don't seep into the workplace environment, then it is impossible for change to occur. Speaking openly about mental health can feel difficult – it may seem easier to 'suffer in silence'. But silence is a choice, and while I know it isn't easy to verbalize our suffering, everyone has a responsibility to speak out, for their own mental health and for the collective culture too.

CASE STUDIES

Chris's story

Stories and experiences of mental health being informally shared within a business can be enough to trigger big investments in mental health and to spark huge changes. Chris Cox is the CEO of Spirit Energy, an oil and gas business with a presence in the UK, Netherlands and Norway. Staff are both office-based and work offshore. Chris became more aware of mental health in the business as he began to hear stories of people being signed off work for their mental health. These stories came to him anecdotally and often through his Executive Assistant, Sharon. She works closely with Chris and plays a role in 'feeling' the company mood. Over time, more and more of these stories were being passed up to him and he wanted to show people in the team that he supported them and that the business had their back.

When I spoke to Chris, I was struck by the simplicity of this and how good it was that Chris knew about the issue of mental health in the first place. He had the relevant information, and whether the people sharing their stories knew it or not, they were building a business case for investing in mental health at Spirit Energy, by talking about their experience. If, for whatever reason, these stories had not been shared in the company, and eventually passed up to Chris, then awareness of mental health would not have happened.

Firstly, the people struggling in this case had to be brave enough to bring their mental health to the attention of their manager and request time off. Secondly, managers or others in the business had to care enough, and not be embarrassed either, to tell others in the company what was happening. From here, the CEO and others were able to see a wider picture of mental health in the company. When it came down to making an investment decision around well-being, for Chris it was simple. They invested hundreds of millions every year in the business, so why not invest a small percentage of that amount in their most important asset, their people? In the end, they didn't have to prepare a fifty-page business case, or even have to go through months and months of approval on mental health, it was a five-minute conversation for Chris with the board, and they decided to commit a seven-figure budget to health and well-being, focusing on mental health, physical health and financial health.

With any success story, there is always more than one thread. What I didn't mention in the Spirit Energy case study is that Chris and the leadership team also started to see the impact on their own performance of focusing on their health and well-being. At a leadership level they were seeing the benefit of focusing on issues surrounding health, and this was part of the fertile ground for an investment in mental health. This isn't uncommon; many of the stories of businesses supercharging their approach to mental health and wider well-being in the workplace come down to conversational awareness of mental health. This only happens if people talk about their own experiences of mental health at work. If it's not being said, then people don't have a chance to hear it and make changes.

When a CEO has good relationships with other members of their team, then they get the opportunity to understand what's happening throughout the workplace. In this case it was Sharon, Chris's Executive Assistant, and others – including Dean, their HR Director – who made it easy for him by sharing information and giving him the chance to see what was happening around mental health in the business. Small, simple actions – like listening, knowing the pulse of the business and informing managers, leadership and the CEO so they were aware of the health of people in the business – led Spirit Energy to make a real commitment to mental health across a business employing 750 people. Everyone took responsibility for their own actions; the people struggling with their mental health shared their experience, and people in management roles shared those stories and passed them up to the top. Without one link in that chain, the wider investment and cultural change around mental health would not have begun.

It only works if everyone plays their part, and it only works if people share their own stories, whatever they may be.

KEY POINTS

- Talking about mental health at work can feel scary.
- Reflect and share your fears in a safe way.
- Be clear on what you want to get out of talking about mental health at work.
- Create the right environment for a conversation.

- Focus on who you feel safe with, not just who you are closest to.
- You might not always get what you want.

Journaling questions

- What's the worst thing that could happen (if you talked about mental health at work)?
- What's been your experience of mental health at work so far?
- Where and to whom do you feel most comfortable talking about your mental health?
- How would the 'perfect' conversation about your mental health go?

9 How to talk to someone about their mental health

I don't want you to do all the talking, I want you to listen too. Being part of a team at work means being in relationships with others. It isn't always about sharing your own experiences of mental health, it's also about listening and connecting with others. You may feel more comfortable talking to someone about their mental health than you do talking about your own experiences and feelings. Through connecting with someone else, you can connect to your own feelings too. You can get a lot from talking to somebody else about their experiences; they can broaden your perspective and develop your empathy, or that person may just be putting into words exactly how you are feeling.

Depending on your perceptiveness or intuition, you may consistently notice the experiences of others. There are many instances when you may want to check in with someone on their mental health, when you may want to bring something up. For example, if you're someone's manager and they're underperforming and you are concerned about their well-being, or if you're a concerned colleague in the same team or a friend at work. Checking in on someone and noticing how they are is part of being human at work.

Be clear on your role

Ask yourself what it is you want from the conversation, or why you may have a desire to check in with a colleague. Is it because you are worried? What are you worried about? What would you like to get out of checking in with someone? Perhaps you'd simply like them to feel they can talk to you. Perhaps you feel like you've been where they are before. Perhaps you are just nosy and you want to know what's going on. This reflection is important, so you have a sense of what your intention is before opening up a conversation with someone on their mental health.

If you have a gut feeling that the person you want to chat to may like some additional support, it's always good to familiarize yourself with whatever support is on offer in your workplace; this could be an employee assistance programme, company healthcare package, or appropriate people at work who can be supportive. If you're checking in with someone about their mental health at work, whatever your role is, you are *not* a counsellor or therapist. Your goal is not to help someone work through their challenges, it's to listen, empathize and connect and, depending on what's going on for them, signpost what could be their next form of support.

Wanting to check in on someone who you think may be struggling is totally normal – and it's also highly likely that you may need support at some stage in your career. Mental health issues are pervasive, and every single one of us is going to struggle with our mental health during our lifetime. It's important to think about what you'd want if you were struggling with your mental health, or what you'd want if someone was to ask you how you are. It's likely that you wouldn't want to be judged, that you'd value knowing that someone cares about you, and you'd want to feel reassured that everyone in the office isn't talking about you behind your back.

Show you care

There's an immense power in showing someone that you care. Letting someone know that you care about them enough to want to talk to them, that you see them, that you have noticed. That, in itself, can be an incredible relief for someone who may feel alone in what they are experiencing. I have found this many times, when getting a WhatsApp message from friends – 'You've been quiet lately, how are you?' – it's so simple, yet it's incredibly heart-warming to be on the receiving end of a message like this.

We can all do this in the workplace. What if someone appears to be doing brilliantly at work? The same applies. You can acknowledge someone, recognize them, ask them what they are having for breakfast. This is all part of connecting and having a more open culture where connecting on a human level is common and part of our business DNA.

Be aware of your fears

You're most likely to be considering talking to someone about their mental health if you think that they may need help. A good place to start is with a reflection on your fears.

- What are you afraid of?
- Are you afraid of getting something wrong?

- What's the worst thing that could happen?
- What other dynamics exist?

If you're the person's manager, you may be concerned that they're not getting their work done and it's impacting the team, yet you'll also have a human concern for how they are feeling. If you are in a caring or helping role in your business, as a manager or in a people-facing role, it's incredibly important that you have your own support at work to take your concerns to. Before you check in on anyone else's mental health, you must have a space for your own anxieties and fears as well.

Say what you see

As a listener, you're the person who's reaching out to someone else to ask, 'How are you?' We can play a really impactful role both as a listener and a mirror. Simply asking the question can be a sign of love and empathy, while sharing what you have noticed in a non-judgemental way can help someone to see themselves in a fresh light, and it can normalize what they're experiencing. Start with, 'I've noticed . . . and I was wondering if . . .' or, 'I've seen that . . . how are things?' In this way you're stating your observations and not jumping to conclusions or making assumptions about what somebody is going through.

Your role isn't to fix someone or try to heal them. Our job is to do that for ourselves. However in a supportive role we can be a listener, or a mirror, and lead someone to find the support they need for themselves. Depending on your own level of self-awareness, you can be empathetic towards whoever you're reaching out to, sharing your own stories of a time when you may have felt the same – or sharing that you can't imagine what they're experiencing because you've not been through it. Again, you're not there to be something you're not; you're a human being and are able to connect with someone on a human-to-human level, and by doing so you can give someone permission to experience what they are feeling.

I'm not exaggerating when I say that a meaningful conversation like this in a workplace environment can be transformative. If someone is really suffering, it could save them from harm or destructive behaviour, or it could act as a turning point for them.

Support yourself

You will know where to draw the line, and how far you can comfortably go, when sharing your experience with someone and listening to someone else's story. I invite you to continue to notice situations where you feel comfortable and where you feel uncomfortable. Your first step could be asking someone at work how they are. Or you may feel more confident naming a regular behaviour you have noticed in someone and simply saying, 'I've noticed . . .'

If you are in a caring role, most likely either in HR or as a manager, I suggest finding more support than I can offer in these pages. Perhaps this is the beginning for you – again, practise in places where you feel safe, and role-model by exploring your own mental health more deeply too. The more we explore ourselves and understand what we need, the more quickly our empathy builds – and our ability to support others grows too. For me, it always comes back to our own level of individual inner work, as I believe we can only support others and connect with others to the extent that we have inquired into our own mental health and our own way of being in this world. The opportunities to connect with and support people at work are great opportunities to create long-lasting, trusting relationships that transcend the workplace. It's these types of conversations that make work more of a community and a place to belong. Being part of that will support the mental health of others and benefit yours in the long run too. You'll get out what you put in.

Be prepared to listen

At work, we can miss the art of connecting quite easily. It's easy to downplay our humanity as we connect with just one aspect of people's lives; we connect with their 'professional self' and we only bring our professional self to the table too. At work it's easy to forget that we're human, before anything else. Lots of businesses lose sight of this and get caught up in workplace politics and culture, missing that it's real human beings, real people, who do the work. How many times are you asked, 'How are you?' and then truly listened to? When you are, how often can you say what you really feel? The answer will depend on lots of things, but what I do know is that it's rare to be asked the question – and it's rarer still to feel able to answer honestly.

CASE STUDIES

Alex's story

Alex Brooks-Johnson joined Guild Care, a 650-person social care charity based in the south of England, as CEO after a period as HR Director. Mental health was immediately one of

Alex's top priorities as part of a wider cultural change where employee well-being and happiness were put high on their agenda. The team were burned-out, giving too much, stuck in an environment where they were simply being allowed to overwork. Given the nature of the business, with a noble mission to care for others, and given their employees' natural inclination to help, there was a dangerous culture of over-giving and of employees not supporting themselves or putting their health first. This was problematic in its own right, with worrying impacts on health, sickness and attrition. Yet the wider cultural problem was a lack of trust in management and leadership, which was creating an underlying low mood within the business.

For Guild Care, the culture around mental health and well-being was specifically the problem because people were feeling tired, overworked, and weren't being looked after or looking after themselves. Alex went straight to people's personal health and well-being as the root of their organizational problems, believing if employees were taking better care of themselves, and that was prioritized by the business, then people would be healthier and more trust would be created across the company too. It was a simple matter of focusing on the health of their employees above all else, and making that a priority for the whole company.

One of the first initiatives Alex introduced as the new CEO was well-being action plans. He mandated that every manager in the company would do regular management check-ins with employees, and as part of them they had to discuss well-being. Firstly, they made sure management one-to-ones were actually happening, and that they were happening regularly. Secondly, they made sure when they did happen, they were quality conversations that focused on an individual's well-being and created the space and permission for conversations about mental health.

To make this happen, Alex put all managers through specific training, and began to see results quickly. Morale across the company began to lift and there was more life and vibrancy within the workforce. Alex began getting more emails from staff, asking questions or just making comments in response to his updates. His employees were even taking the time to ask him how he was doing. The focus on communication and health gave more energy to people, meaning people were more present, focused and able to look beyond themselves and ask others how they were doing too.

There's plenty to admire in the interventions Guild Care brought in. They focused on managers as a really influential population in a workplace, who are in touch with all employees. Managers were given training and support, and a certain quality of management was expected. Managers were also expected to check in directly on mental health and well-being. This meant employees not only got the regularity and support of a check-in with a manager, but were encouraged to talk and think about their own well-being. The intervention here was simple: get managers asking people about their well-being. The execution was diligent, though, too: relevant training for all managers and an expectation that managers brought well-being into their regular one-to-ones. Simple and effective.

The Guild Care story is an example of how a company-wide intervention related to mental health can have a cultural impact quickly across the whole organization. It's refreshingly simple in this case: get managers to have regular conversations with their team and make sure they ask about mental health and well-being. There was a lot of work beforehand by Alex and the leadership team in changing the dynamics and culture right at the top of the business, yet the actual implementation was simple. Company support for mental health in the workplace does not have to be complex or expensive. Getting managers to have conversations with people doesn't cost anything above and beyond what you are already paying people.

The focus on managers is an important one. Managers are highly influential in every company and naturally play a supportive role for people. A good manager can make a huge difference, whereas an unsupportive or difficult relationship with a manager can really impact someone's mental health. Here we see the simple power of taking the time to talk to someone about their mental health, to ask the question and to listen. How great that someone might be telling their manager that they're going to go for a run twice a week for their well-being, and their manager is then following up on that in their next check-in. Initiatives to support mental health in the workplace don't have to be intricate or costly. They can be as simple as management conversations including the question, 'How are you?' and someone truly being listened to.

KEY POINTS

- Make sure you are supporting yourself before you support others.
- Put yourself in their shoes and think what you would need.
- Recognize your own limitations and boundaries.
- Suspend judgement and offer your observations.

Journaling questions

- How would you want someone to talk to you about your mental health?
- What's the worst thing that could happen (by talking to someone about their mental health)?
- What support do *you* need in order to support others?

10 Now you've begun

By exploring your own mental health, sharing your own story, connecting with others, beginning to be more vocal and creating space for mental health conversations at work, you are getting started on your mental health journey – and you may well be doing this at work too. This is foundational work; without the adoption of mental health within the fabric of any workplace, in its core relationships, then no change will happen at all.

By simply prioritizing your own mental health you can make a tangible impact on your life and the life of those around you. From here on, both you and others will feel more able to have conversations about mental health and to let mental health awareness emerge naturally at work. With every conversation, and with every mention of the words 'mental health', the ground for change becomes more fertile. By championing mental health yourself, whether that's through one conversation with one person, or whether you lead a company-wide event, you are participating in cultural change. Culture is the basis for everything that comes after that; the impact you make, however insignificant it may feel, is completely foundational for the mental health approach your workplace decides to take.

Change in mental health at work doesn't just happen to you – although you may be fortunate to be on the receiving end of brilliant initiatives from HR or leaders – these changes are always co-created, and you have a part in that. The HR team create initiatives that they think you may like, so if you don't have a conversation with HR about your mental health, how will someone know what is important to people in the company? You can't be heard if you don't speak up. Our role is to speak up and be part of the mental health cultural movement, in whatever way we can. Whether we lead the change from the front, as a CEO, or we instigate and call for change from our place within the workforce.

There is a lot you can do. You have a responsibility for your own mental health as an individual in your workplace. However, we are all part of a system at work – a corporation, organization, conglomerate, community, family, or whatever you like to call your workplace – we are part of something bigger than just us. Sometimes, we do all we can and show up as all that we are, yet we are still met with resistance. You prioritizing your mental health may mean you quitting your job, and giving your manager feedback as to the reasons why. You prioritizing your mental health may mean cutting back on working longer hours than you have to, until you get the recognition you feel you deserve. Your focus on mental health may mean treating your job as just your job, and finding purpose and fulfilment elsewhere in your life.

You may do all you can and still feel powerless to impact company-wide change because the power to do that may still remain in the hands of the few. I know how disempowering this can feel for those who want more from their work; it can leave us feeling helpless that we can't make the changes we want to, or that we are not being listened to, no matter how hard we try. I know, too, the reality that not everyone can just quit their job and see what happens. Not everyone can tell their boss they've decided to prioritize their mental health so they can't work tomorrow afternoon because they have therapy. As you explore your own mental health, you may see whether your reality is mind-created – as in, it is your way of holding yourself back, based on your limiting beliefs or fears – or whether there is a systemic issue that you simply cannot move past alone.

Your focus on your own story is not to be underestimated, it's a win-win. By prioritizing your mental health, happiness and well-being, you are doing a good thing for yourself, and by telling people, by sharing your journey in any way, you are also inspiring others and making a difference. Doing this in the workplace is powerful because your workplace is a community, like a small town. One impactful conversation around mental health with your boss or colleague can go a long way in the culture, history and traditions of a workplace. Being yourself and focusing on you is the best thing you can do for mental health at work; shining brightly is the most powerful and hopeful thing you can do. That may mean doing things that scare you, making changes in your life or acting differently than you have before. It takes bravery and courage to do that, yet you'll know if the direction you're heading in feels right – and if it does, you'll naturally inspire others. The best way to start the mental health at work movement is to start with your own mental health. Do that, and you'll be part of the movement without even trying.

There is much hope and many examples of change around mental health in the workplace. I know that as you are reading this, you are likely to want something to be different, and you may feel like you are able to make some changes just by focusing on yourself. However, you may need some inspiration too, some hope that change is coming, and some examples of how it has come about. Thankfully, this movement has begun and the revolution is under way. There are leaders and companies that are regarded as shining lights for their approach to mental health in the workplace. It is in their stories that we can see patterns, and we can find lessons that show how mental health can go from being in the dark to being in the light at work.

Your personal mental health journey is intimate to you and inherently unique. Who knows? It may be archery lessons, pottery classes or running that become the changes in your life after exploring or giving more thought to your mental health. Or you may decide to make wholesale changes in your lifestyle, relationships and more. There are diverse choices open to businesses too. Each company needs to find its own unique, authentic path and its own personal approach to mental health in the workplace.

Thankfully, we already have many of those inspirational stories to share, and we will take a look at some of them in Part Four.

Part 4 Mental Health in the Workplace

'If a movement is to have an impact it must belong to those who join it, not those who lead it.'
Simon Sinek

11 Finding the right approach

There's a lot your business can do for mental health at work. I have had the privilege of seeing many businesses transform their approach to mental health in the workplace, and there is much that inspires hope and optimism in me when I see where the world of work is heading in terms of support for mental health. Much like watching an individual grow, develop and flower, watching a business mature its approach to mental health is the same. There's a delicacy and uniqueness, which means that just as every person has a story, every business has a story too. Each business is unique, special and different in its own individual way, which means its approach to mental health in the workplace has different origins and settles into its own unique style. Businesses need their own authentic take on mental health in the workplace, not a bolted-on, tick-box exercise where they just do what they're told to do. We've all seen this: the copied and pasted emails, the small mentions of mental health at the bottom of a long company communication. It's not real, and it's not genuine – it's an afterthought. Businesses that do mental health at work well, all do it their own way: it's real, honest, creative and organic.

Every business has a mental health story. That story may be a negative one of avoidance, of ignorance. Or it may be a positive story of employees being supported when they were struggling the most. Every business has an approach to mental health at work; even a company that doesn't appear to be bothered is still adopting an approach, whether consciously or not.

I'm going to share with you different stories from different businesses which have approached mental health in their workplace in their own unique way. Large businesses, small businesses, in all different sectors. There's no right or wrong way, and there's no exact path for anyone to take. Every business is as unique as the people who are employed in it. We're going to see examples of some of the finest approaches to mental health in the workplace – and, I believe, in the world – and see that change is afoot, change is happening. In some businesses, mental health isn't a taboo subject, mental health is a completely normal part of working life. We're going to look at how that happened, what the conditions were, what the story was, what sparked the change.

My hope is that you'll be inspired and you'll come away with ideas for how you could make an impact. You may realize that your current employer is quite caring, or that they're completely ignorant about the subject. We'll look at these stories and you can take away what resonates with you, and I will share what I have learned from them too. Again, there's no right or wrong approach. Just stories. You will see what you see, and I will say what I see; in that way, we'll connect and, I hope, inspire.

You may have been wondering, 'How will me focusing on my mental health make a difference at work?' So far, we've focused on you, the individual, and your mental health. We've considered how you can make a difference in your own world – in your own circle and personal life. Well, what we will see now is the impact. How the ripples fan out across a whole workplace, a whole company, and how an individual focus on your own mental health can spark change in an entire company – and, eventually, the entire world too.

KEY POINTS

- Every business is different.
- There is no mental health at work playbook.
- Each business must have a creative and organic approach to mental health in the workplace.

Journaling questions

- What is your company approach to mental health at work?
- What does your company do well when it comes to mental health?

12 Leadership

The role of leadership is fundamental when looking at mental health in the workplace. We need leaders to lead, to make change, and to role-model new behaviours that inspire people and redefine workplace culture. However, it is not the role of leadership exclusively to give people what they want. Leaders have a responsibility to listen, while the wider employee base has a responsibility to speak up too. Both must happen at once. In every story both the leadership team and their employees play an invaluable role in co-creating a revolution in mental health in the workplace.

A CEO, in particular, has an incredibly influential role. Often, a CEO's personal relationship with mental health can be enough to completely define an entire business's approach to mental health. Their personal experience may perhaps go some way towards explaining why many businesses and many CEOs seem to show little or no interest in the subject, other than paying it lip service. CEOs are typically under a lot of pressure and have a lot of responsibility; depending on the state of the business or the market they are operating in, they are possibly facing existential threats to their business, which could impact the livelihood of their employees, never mind their mental health. Therefore, depending on the leader and type of business, it can feel difficult for many leaders to focus on mental health; their own may even feel like a luxury to them. As we know, and are continuing to find out, mental health is very personal – and it runs very deep – so if the CEO or other leaders don't want to go there personally, perhaps the company won't be going there either.

If you're a CEO reading this, then you have the power, you have the responsibility to effect change, and it is beyond any doubt that your personal relationship to your mental health is absolutely defining your business's approach to mental health. The stress, the anxiety and the general mood of a CEO sets the tone for an entire business, that's the responsibility of the job. In short, when it comes to mental health at work, a CEO has an incredibly influential role to play.

CASE STUDIES

Brendan's story

Brendan McAtamney is the CEO of UDG Healthcare, a group of healthcare businesses that employs 9,000 people. By his own admission, he wasn't always receptive to conversations around mental health, and typically saw it as some of the 'softer' or the 'fluffier' stuff. Based on his own experience in other businesses, he had one view of work: you come to work, you do what's expected of you, and if you don't do it, you get told. That's not uncommon. That still is the de facto experience for most people at work; work is work and anything else that interrupts the flow of work is probably construed either as an excuse or irrelevant. There's no judgement on that; that's the approach to work we've had for the last hundred years or so, and that may be the approach to work you prefer. When you go to work, you put your work self on and you forget about everything else. You turn your humanity off at work. My guess is, if you're reading this, you don't want that.

Brendan started to see the impact of mental health at first hand. He experienced what it was like to watch someone close to him struggling with their mental health; how they felt, and how he felt in response. It's not a cliché to say his eyes were opened when he realized the impact it was having on them and their life – and on his life too.

After experiencing mental health issues within the family, and with more experience as a CEO, Brendan softened his leadership approach to become more gentle and understanding of what people might be experiencing both inside and outside the workplace. He didn't become less focused on performance, yet he developed an openness to how people might be feeling and their mental health because he knew that impacted their performance. As a result, mental health is firmly on the agenda at UDG Healthcare, not solely down to Brendan as the CEO but because he, in a position of leadership, is open-minded and empathetic. The door is open and his personal awareness of mental health means it's not a business decision to avoid, it's one to take seriously.

If only we could get all CEOs to struggle or to see someone struggle with their mental health. Wouldn't that do the trick? It's undeniable that when a CEO has a personal experience with mental health, then there is a far greater likelihood that mental health will become more important to them within a business environment. When we see mental health clearly, in our own life or someone else's, when we see someone struggle, or someone change, it's so visceral and emotional; it makes such a lasting impression that it's hard to forget. A direct personal experience with mental health will stay with someone for a whole lifetime – and when the person experiencing that is a CEO, the personal impact on them has the opportunity to blossom into an impact across a company of 9,000 people.

Brendan's story is a reminder of why it's important for all of us to focus on our own mental health and the well-being of people in our lives. An awakening to mental health outside the workplace could radically transform our approach to it in the workplace. Even if you're not a CEO, imagine you've been dealing with an emotional situation of mental health within your family life and then, a year later, someone you work with is struggling. There's no doubt you'll be better equipped, more experienced and more empathetic. Personal experiences of mental health lead us to growth; they create opportunities for us both outside and inside work. Experiences with our mental health impact us at our very core, so we carry them with us into every environment we find ourselves in. Yes, if you're a CEO, you have more responsibility and influence, so your impact could be greater. Yet whoever you are, whatever your role, your personal experience with your mental health will impact you in all areas of your life – inside work too. Those in leadership positions play a hugely influential role in shaping company culture towards mental health, and the personal experiences of leaders can define a company's approach to it.

For a long time, there's been a monopolized narrative on what 'good' in our world looks like. Having plenty of money, looking a certain way, having a lot of power, enjoying status, or projecting the right image are just some examples of the dominant story. Within that status quo, mental health hasn't had much opportunity to breathe. Talking about it requires vulnerability and requires us to expose our more fragile, insecure and messy parts. Mental health doesn't always look good, and for a long time society has viewed mental health – or, more broadly, vulnerability – as a sign of weakness. This is one of the reasons why mental health has been swept under the rug. It is why many people have had to suffer in silence or repress their emotional self and personal experiences. These behaviours have been role-modelled by leaders in our society, who feel more pressure and responsibility to show no weakness.

As we go through a transformative shift in mental health, we are going through a shift in leadership too. We are beginning to see a radical shift in leadership that isn't just an aggressive attempt to command and control, but that is nurturing, empowering and gentle. More broadly, I see this as an introduction of more 'feminine' qualities into our world, whereas for a long time our society and leadership our has been dominated by 'masculine' tendencies. I see the introduction of more femininity in leadership, which is paving the way and creating more space for vulnerability and for open conversations about many topics, including mental health.

CASE STUDIES

Jason and Chris's story

Jason Stockwood spent ten years as the CEO of Simply Business, following leadership roles at Match.com and Lastminute.com. At Simply Business, alongside COO Chris Slater, he built a business that disrupted the legacy insurance business very successfully, while creating a brilliant place to work that won the *Sunday Times* Best Places to Work award in consecutive years. Jason is a great example of a leader whose career has seen leadership and management styles change within the last thirty years. In the 1970s and 80s it was 'Show them who's boss'; Alan Sugar saying,

'You're fired,' with a pointed finger. Leadership was about being the biggest alpha male, a lion, king of the jungle.

This aggressive and incredibly macho type of leadership is both fragile for the leader in question and creates a workplace culture based on fear. We're moving away from that, but many of our leaders today still have that voice inside their head, telling them that is how it 'should be done'. For many of us, that's the style of leadership we've seen on films and TV shows, and it's also probably what we're used to from parenting, school and our early experiences in the world of work. For Jason, something as seemingly insignificant as saying, 'I don't know,' in a meeting for the first time as the CEO was a memorable turning point. That doesn't surprise me, as it's a move away from a culture where leaders parade total dominance towards an approach that looks, instead, to nurture and empower those around them.

Chris recalls that at the start of his career he knew no different; work was a 'zero-sum' game where, for you to win, others must lose. That competitive tension, felt throughout the business, was to be expected every day. This view of the workplace assumes it's a jungle; an environment that encourages the survival of the fittest. No wonder people haven't felt able to talk about mental health at work for years, if workplaces have been operating like the Brazilian Amazon. There's been no room for vulnerability, and no space for conversations on mental health, because there's been an underlying fear that you'll be eaten alive – quite simply, your career won't survive.

As a result of their own leadership journey, Jason and Chris led Simply Business with more empathy and compassion, changing the way they showed up as leaders at work – even if, at first, that was new for them too. They set the intention to create a great place in which to work, and to win an award for that, because it was something that they cared about. They wanted to be able to bring more of themselves to work and create a workplace environment where you could make mistakes without fear of ridicule or embarrassment. After winning the *Sunday Times* award two years in a row, they gained public recognition for their approach to leadership, which played a big part in fostering a new and more open culture within the business.

Jason, Chris and Brendan are all excellent examples of leaders who've been on their own personal journey of transformation, moving from type-A, 'win at all costs' leadership to a more open-hearted, vulnerable and compassionate style. Sadly, leaders like Jason, Chris, Brendan – and the others highlighted in this book – remain the exception, not the status quo. For many cultures and institutions, the toxic fear and deep fragility of being found out, and the pursuit of profit at all costs, run deep. The traditional military style of leadership found in the workplace is on its way out, but it's still entrenched; leaders who are approachable, available emotionally, and are unafraid to have honest, vulnerable conversations are still the exception.

Take a look at our global governments and world leaders, and look at what is still the dominant leadership style in the world today. It is mostly 'command and control', with very little focus on empathy, compassion and honesty. On both a global and business level, a change in leadership is under way. It is creating the conditions for more conversations around mental health at work, as well as promoting diversity and challenging other forms of social injustice too.

I am not surprised to see the conversation around mental health at work becoming more prominent as we see more women enter leadership positions. There is a foundational shift occurring in leadership, with a move towards a more holistic approach that encapsulates both the masculine and the feminine. Workplace environments are becoming safe spaces within which to discuss mental health, and permission is being created for people to be more open, honest and vulnerable – bring more of who they are in their personal lives to work. Without a shift in leadership styles – and without leaders role-modelling honesty and a willingness to be vulnerable and compassionate – there will be only stilted and disjointed attempts at an inclusive mental health culture. With open-hearted and open-minded leadership, it is possible for conversations around mental health at work to flourish and for a whole company to evolve together.

KEY POINTS

- Leaders play a fundamental role in creating permission for conversations around mental health.
- A leader's personal relationship with mental health will define their approach at work.
- Leadership styles are in flux and changing.
- Leaders who show vulnerability, are compassionate, empathetic and honest, create safe environments for mental health at work.

Journaling questions

- What qualities do you look for in a leader?
- How could you impact mental health culture in your workplace? What could you do at work?

13 Communication

All businesses need to do is ask. Mental health in the workplace can feel quite ephemeral and hard to grasp. But we've also seen how refreshingly simple it can be: a CEO who cares, managers who listen, mental health advocates who talk more about mental health at work. And yet the next step may be hard to see – especially for larger businesses with lots of employees. The soul work takes time. It's not going to be easy to get the CEO to care more about well-being – that could take years – or it's going to take a long time to roll out the training that gets all managers talking about mental health in the same way.

The problem may not even be with managers; many companies have no idea where the problems are at all. It's always a surprise to me how little people are consulted and how rare it is for someone to be asked, to hear the feedback, and then to do something about it. Again, it sounds simple, doesn't it? Ask someone what their problems are, hear them, commit to doing something, and tell them when it is done. That simple dance of asking, listening and committing is one that creates a lot of trust across an employee base. When a business does this, we can trust the people at the top, we can trust our boss, we can trust leadership, because every time they say they'll do something, they do it. When they ask the question, we know their intention is to make a change. It all starts with asking the question.

When you're dealing with something as complex as mental health, it's pretty silly for leadership to sit in a room wondering what would make people feel better. Their intuition may be bang on, but too often leadership miss the mark because they're out of touch with the feelings of employees. This is why asking the question is key – and, importantly, being willing to hear the answers too.

Communicating across the business sounds simple and obvious. Yet sometimes it doesn't happen, and mental health can be missed.

CASE STUDIES

Neil's story

KFC UK & Ireland have had questions about mental health and emotional wellbeing in their engagement survey for a number of years, yet the responses hadn't stood out as a priority area for them. The questions were there though, and when their employees responded with a growing awareness of their own mental health at work, they listened.

In 2019 they decided to prioritize mental health. They prioritized the question around mental health and really listened to the responses. They asked the question: 'Is KFC an environment that feels safe for your mental health?' This reflected a belief that the working environment had to be psychologically safe for people to do their best work. They received incredibly honest responses from their 28,000 employees across 950 stores, and an incredibly high response rate too, which propelled them into action. They asked the question, they prioritized the question on mental health, and they were ready to hear the responses. There was an open line of communication in the business.

Their Chief People Officer, Neil Piper, pointed out to me that this was one of the defining moments in kick-starting their mental health in the workplace journey. They are a big, global business who can't just turn something around overnight. Yet the hard proof of the engagement survey gave them something tangible to work from, and since that moment Neil and the team have had even more of a reason to focus on mental health at KFC. It's resoundingly simple, when you think about it: they asked and they listened. They communicated.

There are many ways to communicate in a business. When you have 28,000 staff, like Neil Piper, you can do one-to-ones with a close circle, to check the prevailing sentiment, but a company-wide survey like KFC's is very compelling. The only reason really not to do one is because you don't want to hear what you already suspect the answers may be. Yet seeing them in black and white can be the spark that a company needs to get started.

Whatever you choose to do – it can be a company-wide engagement survey, it can be one-to-ones with people, it can be the CEO having open office hours once a week or sending a weekly email – really, what this is about is connecting. It doesn't mean that a company has to let its business be run by vote, it doesn't mean that every decision is made by consulting employees on absolutely everything. There's a value, though, in simply being heard, being listened to, and then understanding why another decision may be being made.

There's no excuse not to be asking the question about mental health at work; it's not hard to create a survey, or to ask questions of smaller groups of staff, depending on the size of the business. What's great about beginning with a question is that it creates a benchmark that can then be quantified; it gives a business something to track its progress against. This isn't rocket science, nor do I believe for a second that businesses do not have the talent and the capability to create engaging mental health policies or to implement mental health strategies in the workplace. This is about priority and focus. If a business took the same creativity and focus it spends on marketing, sales or product, and applied that to employees' mental health, then I am sure things would change quite quickly.

It costs nothing to ask the question, and there's a value in simply asking it. The journey can start there – with one question, and being ready to hear the answers.

KEY POINTS

- Make mental health a priority for the business, and ask the question.
- Find a way to easily communicate with employees.
- Be prepared to listen.
- Create a company engagement survey or conduct a one-to-one with each member of your team on mental health at work.

Journaling questions

- What don't you want to hear?
- What do you already know about mental health at work?

14 Community

Every workplace is a community, whether conscious or not. Work may not feel like a community, but regardless, work is a place where people come together for a common purpose and form relationships in the process. Some businesses consciously create community, others are taking positive steps to move in this direction, while some still see work as just a place to get stuff done, with everything serving that one goal. I see workplaces as offering an opportunity. An opportunity to form meaningful relationships, and a chance to grow together as people too. I believe work can be healing, I believe work can be great for mental health. One way this can happen is if the workplace environment feels like a community; if it is a place where people feel that they belong and are included, where people can bring their whole selves to work, not just their 'professional side'.

Businesses that have a positive and forward-thinking approach to mental health at work often have a workplace with a strong sense of community. We know already that an organic movement towards mental health in the workplace can't happen without protagonists. It can't happen without people lending support, getting involved, or putting their hands up too. It can't happen until people come together at work with a strong sense of community spirit to make a cultural change. That's when everyone, or a significantly large group of people, take mental health at work seriously and take it upon themselves to get involved; when the culture of a company isn't just the responsibility of HR, when it's everyone's responsibility, and people from across all areas of the business feel able to contribute in some way. That contribution could be creating something new or participating in existing initiatives, but either way everyone chips in. That's community – and from community a positive approach to mental health at work often emerges.

CASE STUDIES

Tara's story

Forming a real community at work needs to happen with a group of people, yet it needs a community builder too. At Monzo, Tara Mansfield was that person. Tara is now People Experience Director at Monzo, one of the UK's most recognized and fastest-growing challenger banks. She joined the startup when they were just thirty people, as the Office Manager, and while she was there she took an interest in mental health. She became responsible for leading the company's approach to mental health just by saying yes and grasping the opportunity. Since then, mental health has become a massive part of Monzo's brand, both as an employer and as a bank. Tara was following her intuition and her own desire to be able to talk openly about her own mental health at work, while knowing she could support more people at Monzo too.

Tara wasn't the CEO, or even on the leadership team, at that point. However, very early into her time with the company, she heard the CEO talk in a company-wide meeting about his experience of mental health and therapy. Straight away, it felt as if the permission to be open about mental health was there, right from the top, and with a problem-solving startup attitude, Tara was able to try things and make a difference to their fledgling mental health culture. One of the simple things Tara did was create a mental health channel on their internal communications platform, Slack. This sounds simple, yet through this channel she was able to update people on what Monzo were doing for mental health, and bring together a community of others across the business who shared an interest in it too. Soon people in the business began sharing their stories, sharing their interest in mental health and their gratitude for the openness of the Monzo culture.

Tara played a community-building role in creating the communications channel, yet others in the business played a role by participating too. I can't stress this point enough: everyone can advocate mental health through creation or leadership, yet also through contribution. The employees who decided to contribute to that Slack channel were just as important as Tara in evolving Monzo's mental health culture.

What happened next is even more telling. From that channel, an idea emerged to create some mental health posters for their office. To remind employees that it's okay to talk about mental health. These were cute reminders that mental health is a part of life at Monzo. They even had a suggestions box where people could post what was impacting their mental health. There were other initiatives that didn't always work, but through the creation of community and through storytelling, new mental health initiatives were able to emerge naturally. Monzo's mental health posters were then used in a company blog post that was widely shared, and now Monzo's approach to mental health is a big part of their employer proposition and something lots of potential candidates reference as reasons for applying to work there. The posters were created by people on the Monzo team who also had an interest in mental health. From a personal interest in mental health, to a community within the company and then to an external blog post that adds value to the Monzo brand, this is a beautiful example of a completely organic approach to mental health and how it serves both the employees and the commercial success of the business too.

Monzo even have features within their mobile banking app that cater to people with particular mental health conditions or particular addictions, such as gambling. Here again, we see how employees' interest in mental health, when encouraged to grow organically, is able to impact company culture, recruitment and even product.

I don't know whether the Monzo board talked specifically about making mental health a key part of their brand. I do know that their CEO talking openly about his own mental health to the company speaks volumes and creates an incredible level of psychological safety and permission. Yet that alone isn't the entire story. The story is natural, organic, emergent and empowering. Tara was able to instigate a mini mental health approach in the business, which has gone on to serve employee welfare and the Monzo brand. Perhaps 'approach' isn't quite the right word; it's simply a very natural movement towards something that you desire. Each person at Monzo played a part: the CEO in talking about mental health; Tara in evangelizing mental health; and then other employees in lending a hand and contributing too. There's a real bravery in speaking openly about mental health at work, and there's a real bravery too in saying that you want something. That bravery is shown across the board at Monzo and has resulted in an excellent internal mental health culture and an excellent external brand too. This is a shining example of how mental health can naturally evolve in a company to support employees and be something employees want, and how that can then snowball and begin to shine for the outside world too.

Community doesn't just happen; having a workplace culture where people feel like they can talk openly about mental health doesn't just arise overnight. There are lots of ingredients that have to go into the mix. Yet community can be consciously created, and it can be a priority for a business. Many businesses are beginning to describe their desire for people to bring their whole selves to work; they are consciously moving away from the days when work was simply a place to get the job done, and some workplaces even describe themselves as a family.

In a world dominated by technology, social media and at-home leisure, our society is more connected than ever before, but lonelier and more isolated too. Most of us will spend more time with the people we work with than with our actual friends and family. This highlights the importance of the role of work in our lives: as a community, a place to be, to form relationships, and quite simply a place where we spend 30 per cent of our waking hours. In society in general, there has been a decline in the numbers who regularly attend a place of worship, and less of a focus on local community life. This lack of community across society puts more emphasis on community in the workplace, where people can find a sense of belonging, a support network and a social circle too. Businesses with great mental health cultures create a workplace where there are deep interpersonal relationships, friendships that bolster productivity, and where the working culture transcends the day job. The purpose of the work – the daily rota of tasks to be completed – brings everyone together, yet it's a deeper sense of belonging that keeps everyone there.

With a real sense of community at work, the potential for meaningful conversations, for vulnerability and radical honesty, increases because there's more safety and less fear of being judged. This isn't the experience for a lot of people; many people feel like their work is just a job, nothing more than that. Believing that work can be more than just work doesn't carry with it an expectation that people must work harder, or be totally consumed by their profession. It's an intention that we should all be able to get more out of our work, that workplaces should play a more fundamental role in society, by creating community and providing a source of support for people. I believe most workplaces are a massive missed opportunity. They are places where people come together every day, forming relationships, in order to do a job together. There's huge opportunity and potential for those places to be alive with opportunities for growth, healing and joy.

CASE STUDIES

Claude's story

Some businesses are making their workplace culture a top priority. VaynerMedia is a global media agency founded by Gary Vaynerchuk. At the time of writing, Claude Silver is the world's first Chief Heart Officer there. She works directly with Gary and her role is to 'infuse the business with empathy'. VaynerMedia and Claude go to great lengths to instil psychological safety in their workplace. Claude is intent on creating a culture of safety and permission. Claude's role is to listen and connect deeply with employees, so that they feel seen, heard and valued in the business, every day. Claude's job is to connect with people – and by 'connect' I mean talk to them, hear them and really listen to what is going on across the whole company. If employees are the heart of a business, then Claude is *being* the heart, she is *feeling* the heart and *looking after* the health of the heart.

In other businesses, this role may be called a Chief People Officer or HR Director, yet the Chief Heart Officer role transcends both of those, in a way, because while it still focuses on the typical HR functions, there's also a wider cultural mandate to tune in to the essence of the business and give shape to the 'stuff' that is typically more difficult to quantify. In VaynerMedia's world, the unquantifiable is part of the job of the Chief Heart Officer. Claude spends her time connecting with employees, sometimes just for fifteen minutes; she listens to them, she shares with them, and she creates spaces for open and honest conversations.

Claude shared one example of connecting with an employee and finding out he loved playing the guitar, so she introduced him to three other people in the business who love music. She connected with another employee when they both shared some poetry they had written. How is this work? How is this valuable? I believe it's deeply valuable. When employees are cared for and viewed as more than just employees, there's an acknowledgement that they are more than the job they do. There's an interest in their life outside the workplace: their interests, their passions and who they are. The emotional benefit here for people is huge; when I think about it, I immediately feel more relaxed in my body. It's the feeling that you can be yourself here, that we want you to be yourself and we want you here, all of you. Work immediately becomes more than work, it begins to become a community – a place to be, a place to enjoy spending time – and relationships at work become more than just transactional.

The approaches of both VaynerMedia and Monzo are inspiring and very simple: connect with people. You may not be a full-time Chief Heart Officer, yet anyone can take inspiration from Tara and Claude's stories and start sowing the seeds of a cultural revolution around mental health. Culture is co-created and anyone, absolutely anyone, has the ability to build deeper relationships and truly connect with their colleagues at work. I see businesses like this as the next wave in our relationship with work. As the range of choices proliferates, as people become more educated and informed, and people value their purpose and well-being over their salary, I see workplaces transforming their culture to become even more focused on how they operate as a community. This is nothing new, and many companies have already been doing this, yet I see a shift towards this becoming the primary focus because that is what people want – and people are the lifeblood of any business.

I find myself excited by this move. I see work playing a fundamental societal role in providing belonging, ritual and structure to our lives, where it has been lost in other areas. Work is always more than just work; there's emotion, connection, friendships and more. I see the future as capitalizing on that and making it more explicit, focusing on our humanity at work, not just on what we do. The potential for mental health here is huge because when work becomes more human, or we can bring more of our innate humanity to work, then talking about mental health becomes simple and uncontroversial.

Mental health is a fundamental part of being human, and if a workplace is intent on building a place for all of our humanity, then we will naturally be open about our mental health at work. Anyone can be part of fostering a community at work around mental health; you can lead, instigate or actively participate. It's up to you.

KEY POINTS

- Your workplace is a community.
- Find your tribe at work, create your own support network.
- Put on events for the team around mental health.
- Create internal communications channels for people to talk about mental health.
- Connect with your colleagues about all aspects of their lives, not just about work.
- Actively contribute to and participate in mental health activities and initiatives at work.

Journaling questions

- What does community mean to you?
- What would a sense of belonging be like at work?

15 Creativity

What happens when what's impacting people's mental health in the workplace doesn't have anything to do with 'mental health'? Or when what's impacting employee mental health is more structural – perhaps even existential? Management check-ins, leadership styles, a compassionate CEO, mental health communities at work, and passionate mental health advocates bringing in new mental health initiatives. These are just some of the things we've seen so far from progressive businesses focusing on mental health in the workplace. But I know from my own experience building a business that what impacts people's mental health at work isn't necessarily a result of the workplace culture or the behaviour of the boss, it could be some really frustrating aspect of how the business functions. For example, a certain individual or a certain team could be under an incredible amount of stress as a result of how the business is being operated, and even with all the Zen mindfulness and therapy in the world, people will still feel stressed and unable to fix a systemic issue.

The beauty of mental health in the workplace is that when we look closer and we get curious, we are taken down a rabbit hole that can lead us to very unexpected places. If we suspend our judgement and don't try to immediately fix what we perceive to be the problem, instead asking more questions and looking more closely, it is amazing what we may find. We may simply need to bring in more individual support for people. Or we may uncover some cracks in a business's operating system, or problems within the culture – everything from unfulfilling work to pedantic managers, racism, sexism, low pay, a poor product, company politics, and the list goes on. When we start looking at mental health, we are piecing together various sources of information within our business. Someone's deep stress could either be something individual to them – relating to a situation outside work – or if we look more closely, it could be a sign of a major dysfunction in their particular part of the business. Opening our eyes to the mental health of employees can provide new information on how a business is functioning, and where the operational systems of the business are creating suffering. This information, in turn, will point to a range of potential routes, options and answers, to start tackling the issues identified.

CASE STUDIES

Greg's story

When I first connected with Greg Reed, CMO and CEO at HomeServe, my eyes were opened even wider, to see the full picture of how mental health is not just a cultural issue in a business. Greg joined HomeServe as CMO and eventually became UK CEO of this publicly listed company, which is now up there with Google and Facebook as one of the UK's top places to work. When he joined the business, things weren't so pretty. HomeServe was facing regulatory issues from the Financial Conduct Authority around its product, and there were deep cultural problems in the business; it was a tough place to work – somewhere that people were not proud of. Incentive structures meant that employees were selling products they weren't necessarily 100 per cent behind, and there was a wealth gap between employees and senior management, evidenced by the flashy cars in the car park. There wasn't a lot of love for HomeServe in its communities, which its people experienced first hand, and the general feeling across the business was unease and uncertainty. Greg, along with the CEO at the time, had an insight that if they could make their employees proud of the product they were selling, then people's individual problems, as well as the wider workplace culture, would be positively impacted. Their dual approach was to change the product and change the way people worked, role-modelling a new way of doing business at the same time.

The culture change that led to an improved environment, with fulfilled and happy employees, wasn't changed by bringing in individual benefits or support – although HomeServe do now offer comprehensive mental health support. Greg began at a deeper level, with what people were actually doing each day. Greg would spend a lot of time listening to his employees, seeing himself more as a shepherd guiding and steering from the back, as opposed to driving on from the front. This meant that he constantly placed himself in touch with the most vulnerable individuals or parts of the company, where the most pain, stress, anger or dysfunction were felt.

One of the biggest stresses to HomeServe employees and engineers (those going into someone's home to fix something) was the domestic nature of their product; seeing families who were hugely stressed or angry about a malfunction or breakdown, and sometimes being unable to provide a solution. Customers were often in an emergency situation where, for example, they needed a new boiler in the middle of winter and it would be a painful experience for a HomeServe engineer to have to say, 'No, we can't do that,' or, 'No, you're not covered for that.' Greg realized they had to create a more comprehensive product so that employees felt better about working for HomeServe and about the service they provided.

He introduced an initiative called 'Customer First'. This is an initiative whereby, if a HomeServe employee or engineer cannot solve a customer's problem, they have the right to call into a prearranged daily company meeting the next day with a group of people who are empowered to find a solution. Customer First is referenced in employee feedback on platforms such as Glassdoor to say why HomeServe is such an excellent place to work. Now it means that if a HomeServe engineer can't support a customer when they need it most, they don't have to just say 'no' and leave them stranded at the door.

The ways in which a company can intervene to change the working environment, to foster more happiness and less stress, anxiety and overall suffering, are endlessly creative. In some cases, employees will need more direct mental health support, and no policy or cultural change will impact them. However, in many cases, changing the very nature of the business can have a fundamental influence on how people feel in relation to their work. Greg even got brand-new lighting installed in the HomeServe office because it was so dark in there.

Who knows what your company support may end up looking like? It may be better office chairs, or it may be a new product feature. This is where all the work at the beginning of this book about embedding mental health more naturally into the conversation of the business is so important. Once mental health is there, in the room and part of the company's DNA, then it becomes just another lens through which to look at the business; stress, anxiety, joy, the smiles on people's faces, they all become another frame of reference beyond performance and financial metrics. Once this shift has been made, then creative and organic solutions can be found that will positively impact the working environment, as well as people's overall fulfilment, sense of belonging and happiness at work.

Mental health is not just an 'HR thing'. A business is a living, breathing ecosystem of interconnected, moving parts. The felt experience of any one of those parts is important, and therefore the mental health experience of any individual within the ecosystem is both a rich source of information about the business and a relevant issue for business leaders. The emotional experience of employees can be a gateway for leaders, managers and colleagues to see something that is happening at work, simply by asking the question and listening. If we take the base-level assumption that we all have mental health, every day, all of the time, then we absolutely know that people at work are always sensing and responding to the environment around them. There is always going to be 'stuff', there are always going to be issues, problems and opportunities. This may feel scary, yet it may well be deeply exciting too, filled with thousands of opportunities for growth. This isn't just about fixing problems, either. What if there are populations of employees or teams who are joyous, well balanced and well resourced? What is happening in that part of the business? Those questions could lead to possibilities that transform the workplace and the experience of all the people who work within it.

A focus on the mental health of employees can result in fundamental changes to a business, in how the business functions and how the business is structured. In the same way that there are many different ways to support an individual's mental health, there is also a wide array of company-wide interventions that an employer can instigate that can massively impact that individual's mental health. An employee may be a lot more grateful for a new flexible working policy than a set of massage chairs in the communal area. A better relationship with your manager may improve your mental health a lot more than the workshop on resilience last Thursday. Further, employees may feel under so much stress that the thought of not working for an hour to attend the mental health training the company is providing does not even feel at all possible.

The picture I am painting is that there are countless ways in which a business can improve and change how it actually functions, all of which may have a tangible impact on employees' mental health. If there's a way in which the workplace is operating that is fundamentally broken and is negatively impacting people's happiness at work, then fixing that fundamental problem will be received with far more gratitude than introducing another perk. At its worst, providing mental health benefits without looking at systemic issues can be like rubbing salt in a wound, or providing a plaster that gets ripped off every day in an environment that is consistently harming.

CASE STUDIES

Buurtzorg's story

Buurtzorg have decided to do things very differently. Buurtzorg is a Dutch healthcare business with a completely atypical company structure, one which is self-organized with no hierarchies of power and where teams are completely self-managed. Yes, you read that right: they have no managers, and employees pick their own workload and who they work with too. Their approach to mental health in the workplace has been to look at a completely new way of structuring their entire company, with a belief that typically hierarchical company structures are disempowering and rigid.

Their 15,000 nurses and careworkers work in independent teams where individuals choose who they work with, and between them they pick what they work on, their roles and how they would like to work. Nurses are treated with absolute respect and given a lot of responsibility, autonomy and freedom. As a community healthcare business this is congruent with how they see caring for their patients, by providing holistic care that develops responsibility in the individual alongside community support, not simply focusing on medical interventions. That holistic, empowering message is applied in Buurtzorg's attitude towards its employees. In this brilliant and exceptional case, there are stories of how people's experience at work is so transformative that it leads to a transformation in their personal life outside work. What a gift, what a refreshing tale to hear, so different from the stories I've been telling myself for years about how my work is holding me back. At Buurtzorg individuals have undergone radical personal transformation; their work experience has given them a sense of liberation and freedom, to the extent that the founding CEO, Jos de Blok, was the celebrant at the wedding of one of his employees who was marrying their same-sex partner.

Buurtzorg are a shining light, a company where mental health is woven into the very fabric of the business. They have seized a radical opportunity and made work a place of belonging, healing and transformation because of the way they have decided to structure their organization.

Buurtzorg is a radical example of what I see as a new wave of companies that are purpose driven and do not limit employees' potential to who we can be 'at work'. In these companies the lines between who we are at work and who we are in our personal lives outside the workplace are non-existent; we can simply 'be'. Of course, Buurtzorg is unique and it's important to remember that their model for how employees organize themselves is in line with the purpose and values of their business, down to how they provide their end product. Their business is authentic; the lesson isn't that everyone must be like Buurtzorg and not have managers, as appealing as that may sound. Each business must come up with the answers, the solutions and the change that will be authentic to them. The solutions to establishing a mental health culture at work will look different for every business, and that's okay, that's how it must be.

There are some fairly standard practices: therapy, coaching, training, manager training sessions, and more. Yet their adoption, as well as the wider cultural and structural setting, has to be tailored to fit the individual business and its unique personality. Buurtzorg has chosen a radical company structure that works for them; perhaps many other businesses will be inspired to follow their example. The building blocks that create a supportive environment for mental health are many and varied. They could include the company structure, a set of benefits, leadership styles, and more. For Buurtzorg the answer has been to remove power hierarchies and give employees an exceptional level of autonomy, yet for some businesses that may create more anxiety and not work at all.

I want us to move away from looking for a silver bullet and for how it 'should' be done, and begin being more curious about what could be different in our workplace. I want us to look inside for our answers, not only at examples from outside. As we do this, we'll be organic and we'll be creative in how we change our approaches to mental health at work.

KEY POINTS

- Any part of a business can impact employee mental health.
- Company structure, product or processes impact people's mental health.
- Every business needs to be creative and listen to their internal systems.
- Be open-minded about what is causing pain, frustration or friction in the business.
- Use mental health and people's feelings at work as another form of data and information for the business.

Journaling questions

- Where is the most stress at work?
- What would make work ten times better?

16 Investment

It's time to put your money where your heart is. I have heard of workplaces where you have to bring in your own tea bags and where there is one microwave between a hundred employees. I've been in workplaces where their canteen is like a Michelin-starred restaurant. Or where there are table tennis tables, comfy chairs, on-site masseuses, and all sorts of additional comforts. The level of investment in the working environment of any business varies widely, from very low to very high, and often coincides with industry standards and the competition for talent in that industry.

The technology industry invests very heavily in employee perks, benefits and well-being because demand for software engineers is so high. The war for talent is obvious and understandable, so creating an incredible workplace environment, with all the perks and benefits someone could ever need, can make an employer stand out from the crowd. Investment in mental health and well-being benefits can be viewed in the same way; it's an obvious argument that someone may choose to join a business with better mental health and well-being benefits than another. Yet what are the other impacts of investing in someone's mental health at work?

We can make the case for almost any employee perk – for example, holidays. People love holidays and they make people happy, so why don't we pay for our employees to go on holiday? The list goes on – and who knows where it will stop, as the convergence of work, our personal and family lives continues? Physical health benefits are a more obvious investment. But why have fruit in the office, or why subsidize gym memberships? Well, healthy staff are less likely to be sick, which is good for business, and they may also be more productive, with better morale too. Mental health, though, is even more closely linked to our life at work because our mental health often defines how productive we are at work.

Investment in a range of health benefits and perks makes logical sense. An investment in the mental health of employees seems to underpin the welfare of an entire employee base, so what happens if you do just that? It's still early days, but many businesses now are beginning to dramatically increase their investment in benefits which support their employees' mental health and well-being. It's always going to be hard to attribute or quantify positive impacts, or find cause and effect, in mental health. Yet there are many businesses continuing to make these investments in the belief that it's the right thing to do, and trusting to their intuition that it pays off in the long-term as well.

CASE STUDIES

Katy's story

Social Chain is a media business with offices in Manchester, London and New York. It is a young business with around 200 staff and has always placed employee happiness at the centre of its strategy, values and focus. Katy Leeson is the Managing Director and as well as being very open, forthcoming and approachable about her own mental health, she has worked hard with the leadership team and two founders to establish a workplace culture and overall operation that cares for employee health and happiness as a priority. The company has an on-site therapist, an in-house life coach, a brilliant office with everything anyone could ever need, and a full-time Head of Happiness too. Social Chain has put the time and money into investing in health and happiness for its employees. It has created a memorable working experience for people who join the team and fostered loyalty, with lower than average attrition rates for the industry.

Katy thinks this focus on health and happiness has played a fundamental part in enabling Social Chain to thrive during the Covid-19 pandemic, despite the two founders leaving the business, and spurring it on to have its most profitable quarter ever when we last spoke. It's almost impossible to attribute this directly, as there's no conversion rate when it comes down to the link between someone's mental health and performance. Yet to Katy, who's the MD looking at the whole picture, its long-term approach of investing in people is paying dividends in the face of really tough and unprecedented working circumstances.

I see it really plainly too. I see that people are inherently good and when treated well, with respect, over time they will return that and more. People want to do their best work. There's an outdated employee vs employer story, where one is trying to take as much as possible from the other. I think that's an old-fashioned Victorian workhouse belief, and what people really want is to work as equals and be fairly treated and rewarded. I believe most people want to do their best work and that's why they join a company, so if they are treated well they'll thrive and try their hardest. The Social Chain story makes perfect sense to me; it has treated people brilliantly, invested in people over time, and asked for employees to do their best work with it. Now that long-term investment in employees is paying off, especially when things get hard, because people want to be there, and it has generated a level of trust and loyalty to the business.

It's back to basics again. Treat people well. Mental health is a vital part of people's well-being, so seeing mental health as an intrinsic part of humanity – and therefore an intrinsic part of any workplace – will support people to thrive at work. There has to be the buy-in at the very heart of the company, and there has to be a moral belief that the company has a duty to their employees that goes beyond their role in the workplace. Truthfully, some businesses, boards and leaders may not see the world this way. In my view, those businesses will slowly die as people choose to leave them, or they are disrupted by more innovative businesses with a more holistic approach to their employees' welfare. There is a level of love and trust that must exist, where the business is willing to care for employees and expect nothing more in return than the execution of the job they have been hired to do. If a business holds that belief and expects nothing in return, simply because they believe it to be right, it is highly likely their employees will pay them back over time.

The commercial story is there too: a better employer brand, better candidate attraction, decreased attrition and lower sickness rates across the business. That's just the rational stuff. In the soul of the business there's increased trust, loyalty, safety, belonging, creativity and diversity, which of course are much more difficult to track over time. The story for investing in employees is there and always has been; it's the cultural stigma of mental health that has been in the way. As more and more businesses like Social Chain continue to grow, then investing heavily in the mental health of employees will move from being the exception to becoming the status quo. I'm pleased to say I believe we are already on that path.

CASE STUDIES

Simon's story

Octopus Group are another example of a company making an exceptional level of investment in their team, and achieving exceptional results too. With more than 1,000 people employed across 6 different businesses, including real estate, investments, energy and financial services, they are investing heavily in their employees, and at scale. Simon Rogerson is the founder and CEO there, who I've had the pleasure of getting to know over the last few years. Their decision to invest in their staff is intimately linked to a worldview held by Simon and the entire Octopus team that encapsulates how they see great business. For Simon, most businesses waste their effort trying to be the smartest, the fastest and the most adaptable in the market; they spend their time thinking about how they can outperform and beat the competition. Yet for Simon and the Octopus Group, they believe in out-behaving their competition and believe that this is a sustainable competitive advantage that they are always in control of. 'Great business is simply about how you make your customers feel. This, in turn, comes from your people.'

This core belief – that great business is about how you make your customers feel – is deeply ingrained in the business. With this as the grounding philosophy, the decision to invest in the health and well-being of Octopus employees starts to feel simple. If their guiding belief is that they want to out-behave their competition and make their customers feel great, it makes logical sense that they have to make their employees feel great too and do everything in their power to ensure their people are happy. Mental health and the problems people face inside and outside work are a big part of someone's overall happiness. So, in Simon's opinion, it's their responsibility to help people in whatever way they can with their mental health.

Mental health isn't an add-on, it's not a perk. It's not even a nice-to-have. It's an absolute fundamental to our lives – and since people are the beating heart of any business, it's a fundamental in every business too. Mental health is at the heart of every individual, therefore it is always at the heart of every company. Mental health at work is a strategic focus, it's a priority and it is deeply linked to every facet of a company's ecosystem: how employees feel, how customers are treated, how a company functions, how leaders show up and operate.

Octopus shows in elegant simplicity that a focus on mental health is both human and commercial at the same time. I love that one of their values is being straightforward because it is so straightforward. Treat employees well, look after employees and care for them, and that will spread out to customers, stakeholders and clients. That is beautifully straightforward and beautifully simple. It has to be true, though; it has to be real. Those values can't be fake and just written on the wall, they have to be lived out – and clearly, in the case of Octopus, they are. It looks like it's working too, with Octopus Energy – just one of Octopus's six businesses in the group – growing to be valued at £2bn after being founded in 2015. Alongside the success of

Social Chain and the other businesses we've highlighted in this book, the focus and the investment in mental health at work are great for people, and great for business too.

KEY POINTS

- Investing in employee mental health creates loyalty, trust and good results long-term.
- Invest in benefits that support people's mental health at work.
- Treat people well and they will do their best work.
- Your people are your greatest asset.
- Happy employees will create happy customers.
- Mental health really matters to your employees, so it needs to really matter to your business.

Journaling questions

- What would investing in mental health at work look like?
- What investment would support employee mental health the most?

17 There's nothing stopping you now

There are many different ways in which we can work on our own mental health, from coaching, therapy, yoga, to a whole host of other activities or interventions. The same applies to businesses; there are an infinite number of ways in which an approach to mental health can originate in the workplace, and a limitless number of possible architectures or elegant approaches that can emerge. The question 'What supports mental health?' will continue to live on – and long may it do so. I have highlighted some of the stories, businesses and leaders who are at the forefront of mental health at work. There are direct individual interventions that are becoming commonplace, both inside and outside the workplace, and I have shared stories of how companies have changed their behaviour systemically to impact their employees' mental health. There is hope because there are brilliant leaders and brilliant companies making mental health in the workplace look easy. There is hope, too, because there is so much we can do to impact the lives of those around us at work.

Much of the change I have documented and many of these stories I have told sound, on paper, relatively simple. Any story, on paper, sounds simple because it is being told after the fact. What much of these stories don't capture is what it was like for the individuals in the moment; we're just seeing them now they've arrived at their destination. What these stories do, though, is provide hope and living proof that change is coming – and that change is a real possibility too.

You may be experiencing a range of emotions as you read this – anywhere from exasperation to joy, from despair to hope – and I invite you now to check in with yourself and see how you feel as you reach this stage in the book. I certainly feel hopeful because I know that the support is out there, the interventions exist, the tools and the practices are readily available, and we have role models to look towards. The reality is that many of the practices I have outlined, from individual support to company-wide initiatives, have always existed, or have existed for a very long time. The difference isn't in the provision of solutions or forms of support, it's that we are ready to access them and we are here, right now, having this conversation.

The time is now, and it has been now for a long while. That's not a nudge to rush to get started. It's a reminder that we have been the ones holding ourselves back with mental health – our own pain, our own fear, our own doubts – and it is time for all of us to move past those together. The support is out there for people to be trained, to work through their issues, to grow and to transform, and the opportunities are there for us to change the way we work to create workplaces that are fundamentally healthy.

I find this hugely exciting and a huge relief. It's liberating to know that the tools are there for us, the answers are there, we just haven't been asking the right questions. Not one of the individual stories we have covered is necessarily better or worse than any other; they all have their own benefits, and their own costs too. Company-wide operational or systemic changes are probably the hardest to implement, depending on the agility and desire for change within the organization. It may be easier to find the budget for an on-site therapist than it is to get the marketing team to do things a little differently – who knows? I decided to share the stories with you so that you can take away from them what resonates with you and is relevant to your individual situation.

I could have written a 10-step guide, but it would be redundant within a year as the world, no doubt, changes again. Or it would feel like another thing you're not doing enough of. These stories are here to inspire you, to give you hope, and to stay with you so that you can create your own journey. Whoever you are, you will relate to them differently. If you are a CEO, you may feel inspired to put something new on the next board meeting agenda; if you're in HR, you may feel clearer on the moves you can make; if you are in a sales role, you may feel excited about exploring your own mental health more. These stories of mental health and mental health at work are there for you to connect with, in whatever way is relevant for you.

If you take nothing else away from this book, know that the mental health movement is happening and is transforming the way we work.

There is a revolution on the way.

Part 5 The Movement

18 It's a life's work

> Be a light so bright that you fire up those around you.

Our focus on mental health at work is absolutely critical in the wider cultural movement around mental health. Mental health is deeply complex, embedded firmly within ourselves, entangled in our work, relationships, families, friends and more. There is a mental health movement on the way and our workplace can be where the movement begins to take shape.

We have started our journey in the pages of this book, and wherever it takes you, I will be pleased. I hope you read more about the subject of mental health, have more conversations, or try something out and take a risk. I hope you take your own step forward, whatever that may be. There are no short cuts, and there is no silver bullet, either in our personal lives or at work. To create organic, sustained and long-term change, your actions need to feel bold, challenging and with an edge of vulnerability. Therein lies growth. When you cover up the cracks, when you tick the boxes, there's no growth and there's no healing.

This may already be, or may have become, your life's work. You may already have devoted many years of your life to the issues raised in this book, and much of what we've shared here may have resonated with you, raising a knowing smile or a nod. Or a white-hot passion within you may have begun to burn brightly. What we have shared here are the seeds of what is a constant process, both inside and outside of work. For you this may be the beginning, or simply more information to accompany you on the path you are already travelling. If you still have the pressure of an end destination in sight, try to drop it, let it go, and revel in the feeling that rather than needing to be somewhere other than where you are, you are already there. When it comes to mental health, the only place to be is here.

This is the journey of a lifetime, with constancy and continuation. The process will always be to listen, to be honest, to be open, to be curious, to be brave and to ask the questions. That type of life is a choice of how to be, and the content – whether at your place of work or at home – will continue to change. Your workplace environment will also continue to change: a new job, a new boss, a new employer. Whatever the differences may be, mental health at work will not be solved or fixed. There will always be new issues, challenges and opportunities.

The journey is deep, existential and takes us to the very essence of our being and consciousness. This book focuses on the workplace, yet in the light of mental health, the workplace simply falls away to become another group or community that we are part of. All the walls, the conventions, the stories we have told ourselves fall away, the money, the status, the do's and don'ts – they all look different in the light of mental health. In many ways, nothing is more important than this: this is it, this is mental health, this is life. This book could have been called *Life at Work*, as there's little difference. Mental health at work is the taste test of the quality of our life at work – and I don't mean life as in our mortgage, money in the bank, or other material possessions. I mean our *being* at work, how we are at work. This is so important and this focus on mental health at work is increasingly important too, given the role that our professional life plays in the world.

In a world where the majority of our news is negative, where society seems to feed on hate, on problems and on negativity, there is light if we choose to see it. If we choose to ask, 'What is right?' rather than focusing constantly on what is wrong. There is much to be hopeful about, much that we can see and already celebrate, inside and outside ourselves. We can continue moving towards the light. There are signs of change, and signs of great flowers blossoming; companies that look, think and act differently. Companies whose very existence is a beacon of hope, a light shining brightly that can guide us. Leaders who are inspiring in their honesty, courage, values and integrity. There is always hope.

We are still in the foothills of this journey. We have a long way to go and the evolutionary shift that is undoubtedly coming will take time. It will likely take a generation. We are at a moment when we are transitioning from one way of being to another. A huge societal, global transition. How that impacts the way we work is going to be profound, yet it is not going to be instantaneous. There will be time for leaders to ask questions, to prioritize purpose over profit, time for businesses to see employee health as an urgent priority, and time for people to adjust to feeling able to be truly honest at work. This movement is already happening. What may feel hard is that it's not happening quickly enough – we're impatient, and we want it to happen right now.

While the talk of a movement, or a new wave of mental health at work, may sound like a destination or an end point in itself, I can assure you it won't be. I have faith that it will be different, and better in many ways than our experience in this moment, yet it won't be perfect, it won't end pain or suffering. I do believe we are moving towards a way of being that could feel a lot more authentic, where energy does not have to be expended hiding our true selves, faking it or wearing a mask. Where feelings may be openly shared and where honesty is valued as the status quo, and not surprising. Our problems won't go away, yet I do believe we can lessen their impact on us, by taking away the internal pressure of judgement, shame and resistance. I hope we can move towards a greater acceptance of what is happening in the present moment; not resisting it, avoiding it or trying to dress it up. We are on a path towards that, and work has a role to play in it, just as we have a role to play while we are at work. Work is where we spend most of our time connecting to others, where many of the interpersonal relationships in our lives are formed. Every one of us has a role to play in our work community, everyone has the power to make a difference in some small way, and I believe everyone must.

In thirty years we will look back with shock, horror – and, I hope, a smile – at how we used to approach mental health as a society. I hope I'll be a doddering old man and my grandkids will say to me in an incredulous tone, '*What?* You never used to talk about how you feel! How did you survive?' Just as I can't believe that people used to smoke indoors, or people used to drink and drive, and very few people exercised for health or leisure, I am certain the same surprise will be felt when we consider our archaic and antiquated view of mental health.

I believe what we are part of is a revolution in consciousness, and mental health is at the centre of it. There is an awakening happening, both within us individually and on a collective level. A move from unconscious behaviour – mindless, ego-centred action – towards conscious, heart-led behaviour that is respectful of our place in the world. This movement is powered by mental health and is already linked with changes in attitudes to gender equality, racial equality and the climate crisis. It starts at the individual, human level, waking up to the world around us, to the pain, suffering and injustice, and looking for change, for another way of living. I believe a shift in perception and attitudes towards mental health is going to fuel movements and change across broad areas in our society. How we see ourselves and our own part in the world, how we feel about ourselves and the quality of our being, will fundamentally impact the way we live, the choices we make, the things we buy, the causes we care about and our environmental footprint. A deep, sustained focus on mental health at a collective level will fundamentally change our entire world for the better.

At work, the benefits of the change that is coming are stark and obvious: companies treating employees like human beings, with trust, respect and holistic care; leaders making decisions that take account of the health of the planet, not just financial outcomes; business owners and entrepreneurs starting companies with deeper societal and humanitarian missions.

When individuals shift how they perceive their own lives, and how they prioritize their mental health, then our outlook and worldview will shift entirely. From a grassroots, ground-up, collective level the whole world is going to change. You are a part of that movement and this revolution. You are beginning to consciously engage in it. I am incredibly grateful for the opportunity to be alive at this time in history and believe we have been given a huge chance to be part of an inflection point in the transformation of humanity. We truly are writing history as we speak, and the revolution in mental health at work is an important part of that history. How we work – the selves we bring to the workplace and how we are with one another – is a defining part of the cultural transformation in mental health.

I feel excited, hopeful and yet remain a little fearful. I'm excited for the possibilities of a new world where mental health is talked about in the same way as our physical health. Hopeful that I see this change coming. A little fearful that I may not live to see the end of the proverbial rat race that humanity seems trapped in. Yet the excitement and hope are more than enough to propel me forward, and the fear is a grounding reminder of where we are today. I know this is my mission: to be part of this movement. I don't know the exact route I will take, but I know the horizon I am walking towards and I hope many of you will decide to walk towards it too.

What I do know is that, together, we'll get there.

Thank you for taking this step with me.

Publisher's note

This book is not intended to be a substitute for professional mental health support delivered by a qualified mental health practitioner. Nor is it a self-help book based on proven mental health interventions. This book does not claim to provide mental health support, and neither the author nor the publisher is responsible or liable for your mental health as a reader of this book. You are responsible for sourcing the support you need from the right places. It is our hope that you will feel better equipped to do so because of this book.

Acknowledgements

My mental health and views of mental health have been influenced by many people I have worked with over the years, yet none more so than Ben Graham, who was one of the first psychotherapists and coaches I ever had the great fortune of working with. Ben's approach to mental health, his gestalt psychotherapy training and work with me directly have had an enormous impact on the writing of this book.

While not explicitly referenced in the book, the gestalt approach to mental health has been very much in the background of my writing. I'd like to thank the Metanoia Institute and the organization Relational Change for indirectly influencing this work.

If I were a coach or a therapist, I'd have a supervisor. If I were lucky enough, I'd have Kate Glenholmes as my supervisor. I'd like to thank Kate for her time spent with me on this book, her support, challenge and mentorship. Particularly, I'd like to thank her for supporting my confidence and credibility in writing a mental health book, and explicitly for speaking to topics such as suicide directly.

I would also like to thank Felicity Hodkinson for her support and time spent with me on the sections of the book on talking to others about your mental health, and for the years of coaching too.

I did not write this alone – no, I mean I literally did not write this book alone. The majority of this book was written in a community with others. I wrote the book with the Writers' Hour community, led by Matt and Parul, where I spent many mornings and afternoons silently writing on a Zoom call with hundreds of people. Through this community I was able to find accountability and a shared sense of purpose, and that feeling of belonging helped me immensely in completing the book.

George Bell, George Bettany and Sarah Lloyd were the three people willing to read this book in draft format and give me extensive feedback at short notice. I'd like to say thank you to George Bell for the detailed feedback and a constant show of support, which gave me the self-belief to keep writing. To GB, thank you for the WhatsApps and the voice notes and the claim that this is 'the best mental health book ever written': that's only a few snippets of the infectious enthusiasm that light up my life every day. To Sarah, who this book is dedicated to, I can't begin to say thank you enough for supporting me as a founder, author and fiancée who often forgets that we've agreed to go on a walk this evening.

One of the main breakthroughs in the structure of this book came over a Christmas period when I was staying at my parents'. Thanks, Mum and Dad, for giving me the space and time to walk around the kitchen talking at you. Thank you for giving me the life, love and belief that I could even write a book.

Thank you to all those I have interviewed who are referenced directly in the book. Your stories, words and interviews were inspiring, and I am pleased they're now in print for others to read. Thank you for your time and, more importantly, for your work that I've had the opportunity to shine a light on.

Thank you to the whole Sanctus team, who continue to make waves in the mental-health-at-work revolution. You are all an inspiration to me, and without Sanctus as a platform I doubt I'd have had the opportunity to write this book. Which I hope elevates our work and the cause of mental health as a whole.

Last, but certainly not least, I'd like to thank all my mates – you know who you are. I toyed with writing out all your names but I'm not sure I have the space. If you are reading this, then you'll know I mean you. Thank you for the support, the genuine congratulations, the check-ins on how it's all going, and the comments that bring me down to earth and raise me up too.

And finally, finally a huge thank you to the team at Penguin for this opportunity and to my editor, Celia, for responding to the frantic WhatsApp messages while soothing my concerns too.

Cheers,
James x

Further resources

This book is intended to start you on your mental health journey, and I hope you are well satisfied. Yet I'm still happy if this was just your starter and you're now up for a main course. I encourage you to set out on your own exploration and to lean into your own intuition when sourcing books and practitioners to continue your adventure into mental health.

This book may have opened a door into your own mental health and you may feel like you need more support. If that level of support feels urgent and you feel as if you may be a risk to yourself or others right now, then please call the emergency services or call a helpline such as the Samaritans in the UK on 116 123.

You may be left feeling like you want more support, but don't know where to turn. There are lots of different kinds of mental health support available that are free, low cost or specialize in addressing specific areas of mental health or a variety of cultural backgrounds. We haven't covered absolutely everything but the Sanctus Directory is a good place to go if you are looking for different forms of mental health support. You'll find it on https://sanctus.io/directory.

Remember, too, some of the guidance in this book about finding spaces where you feel safe, whether with friends, family members or colleagues. Please reach out and start conversations where you feel safe enough to do so. If there is nobody in your immediate circle, then use the helplines or other organizations above; they are easy to access.

The feelings you are left with after reading this book could also be curiosity and excitement; you may want to deepen your experiences around mental health by working with a coach or therapist. Reach out to friends for recommendations. Share your experience and journey with others, as we recommended at the start, and see where that takes you.

Finally, your workplace is likely to have some mental health support. Reach out, find out what it is and use it. You are likely to have an EAP (employee assistance programme) or possibly health insurance; you will only find the right support for you by asking the question and reaching out. If you are championing mental health in your workplace and are interested in the work Sanctus does, by partnering with businesses to create safe spaces for employees to explore their mental health, then please reach out to us through our website at https://sanctus.io.

We'd love to hear from you.

Index